The Kerala Kitchen

The Kerala Kitchen

Recipes and Recollections from the Syrian Christians of South India

Expanded Edition

Lathika George

Illustrations by Latha George Pottenkulam
Foreword by Abraham Verghese

HIPPOCRENE BOOKS, INC.
New York

Expanded Edition, 2023

Book and cover design by Pooja Pottenkulam.
Photography by Salim Pushpanath.

For more information, address:

HIPPOCRENE BOOKS, INC.
171 Madison Avenue
New York, NY 10016
www.hippocrenebooks.com

Previous edition ISBNS:
ISBN-13: 978-0-7818-1184-2 (hardcover)
ISBN-13: 978-0-7818-1344-0 (paperback)

Cataloging-in-Publication Data available from the Library of Congress

ISBN-13: 978-0-7818-1444-7

Printed in the United States of America.

For my mother Thangamma
and
my sister Shashi

Contents

Recollections of Kerala

South India

Arabian
Sea

K
E
R
A
L
A

Calicut

Trichur

Malayattoor

Kodangallur

Injithotti Periyar
Kothamangalam

Cochin
(Mattanchery
Koonen Kurisu)

Palai

Thycattuchery

Manimala

Kottayam Kanjirapalli

Alleppey R.block

Pamba Nilackal

Kuttanad
Wetlands
(Palathuruthy,
Nedumudi and
Kidangara ferries)

Achankovil

N
W   E
S

Quilon

Foreword

by Abraham Verghese

When I first read *The Kerala Kitchen* by Lathika George, I remember feeling as though I'd stumbled onto a treasure in my grandmother's storeroom or *ara*, the strongroom where she kept her paddy and her jewelry. The dishes described in the book were the same delectable ones that my grandmother and my mother used to make—staples of every Kerala household, both in Kerala and its far-flung diaspora. But what makes the book you are holding so different than the usual cookbook (and I have a collection quite out of proportion to my culinary skills) are the wonderful narrative asides, the historical tidbits, and the gorgeous photographs that are interspersed between the recipes. I was delighted by the author's childhood memories of visits to her grandparents and the personal connection and background that informs each dish. On my first reading—and I read the book cover to cover, as if it were a novel—I realized that Lathika George is not just a wonderful cook, but also a brilliant writer and storyteller. In these pages you have much more than a cookbook.

Kerala is a unique coastal strip of land on the southwest tip of India, walled off for centuries from the rest of the country by a great mountain range that runs parallel to the coast, the Western Ghats. On the fertile slopes of these mountains, spices such as pepper and cardamom grow wild like weeds. Forty-four rivers stream down from the mountain ranges to the coast where instead of estuaries they form a latticework of backwaters, lakes, ponds, lagoons, and miles and miles of waterways. This unique geography makes water a major mode of transport, commerce, and social life in Kerala; not surprisingly, water has tremendously influenced the culture of its people as well as its cuisine. (It's the reason that I made sure to put the word "water" into the title of my novel set in Kerala, *The Covenant of Water*.) The abundance of water makes for a lush and verdant landscape dotted with coconut palms, rice paddies, tea and rubber estates, and of course the cultivation of spices. For many centuries Arab traders sailed on their *dhows* to the "Spice Coast" to buy spices; when the tradewinds reversed they carried their treasures of cloves, cinnamon, pepper, and other spices to sell for huge profits in Palestine to merchants from Europe. Europeans used these spices for all kinds of strange purposes, from countering the noxious odors emanating from the straw-packed floors of their dwellings, to rubbing spices on parts of their body for medicinal and libidinous purposes; it somehow never occurred to them to grind spices together and fry them with shallots, ginger, and garlic to make a curry in which to cook fish or fowl. In this book you'll discover how over the centuries Keralites have refined the use of spices to produce the variety of dishes described.

In the years since I first came across *The Kerala Kitchen*, I've given away many copies to friends and relatives. I was also privileged to finally meet and visit with the author. In the decade it took me to write *The Covenant of Water*, Lathika was hugely helpful in my research, answering countless emails, sharing anecdotes and family lore, and introducing me to others who proved to be great resources. She must have felt sorry for my solitary labor because she even shared with me some quick recipes such as "bachelor chicken" which you won't find in this book. It remains one of my go-to dishes.

My copy of *The Kerala Kitchen* has notes scribbled in it and has turmeric stains on certain pages. Now it's your turn to enjoy. So line up your spices, ready your grated coconut and go to it. You are in for both a literary and gastronomic treat.

—Abraham Verghese

Abraham Verghese is a physician and writer and holds the Linda R. Meier and Joan F. Lane Provostial Professorship at Stanford University, Palo Alto, CA. He is the author of the bestselling novels, Cutting for Stone *and* The Covenant of Water.

Introduction

Long before the time of Christ, the lure of spices took traders and seafarers to the verdant coast of Kerala on the southern tip of India. The port of Cranganore was bustling with Greeks, Arabs, Syrians, Jews, and Chinese merchants who lived in harmony with the people of the region. It was on one of these trading vessels, plying between Alexandria and the Malabar Coast, that Saint Thomas the Apostle is believed to have arrived in AD 52. He eventually established one of the oldest surviving Christian communities in the world, the Syrian Christians of Kerala.

The present-day Syrian Christians are a distinct community with deep roots in the culture and culinary traditions of their forefathers. The cuisine truly embodies the ethos of Kerala and its people: drawing upon the various cultures that have influenced them, it fully exploits the bounty of Kerala. Meals are a celebration of the spices, herbs, seafood, meats, pulses, grains, nuts, and every edible leaf and seed that grows in this fertile land. Through the centuries, mothers have taught their daughters how to use herbs and spices with just the right blend, so that they enhance the essential flavor of the main ingredients without overpowering them.

Though I grew up in Bombay, I was introduced to the food of my Syrian Christian ancestors at an early age. My mother, Thangamma, like most mothers around the world, believed that the strongest bonds between children and their culture are forged through food and the preparation of meals. To ensure that we kept in touch with our Malayali roots, we were raised on a diet of *Puttu* (Steamed Rice Cake), *Meen Vevichathu* (Fish Curry simmered in a clay pot), *Erachi Olathiathu* (Stir-fried Beef), and other staple Syrian Christian dishes. As few Malayali ingredients were available in grocery stores in Bombay, the trucks from Kerala that supplied foam-rubber sheets to our family's mattress-manufacturing factory in Bombay also brought fresh supplies of parboiled red rice, plantains, bananas, tapioca, rice flour, and *palaharams* (sweet and savory snacks). One year, in her enthusiasm for authentic produce, my mother even raised a patch of red country rice in our backyard in suburban Bombay.

Summer vacations spent visiting the extended family in Kerala would strengthen these bonds even further. Each year we spent a month travelling through the lush countryside, starting from Cochin to the old seaport of Allepey then on to the backwaters of Kuttanad. From there we would proceed to Kottayam and then up the hills to the rubber estates in Kanjirapally. These journeys were punctuated by stops at little teashops, picnic lunches by the river, and memorable feasts at family homes. We returned to Bombay replete with new experiences and memories of delicious food cooked in smoky country hearths.

1

There are moments that stay with you forever, evoked by the foods we prepare, dishes which recall the stories that grew around their enjoyment. My mother was a great storyteller. Tales of family intrigues and events in Kerala were accompanied by recipes, fables, and songs, all part of her repertoire of bedtime stories. Often she would bring out her old harmonium and sing to us in her low, well-modulated voice, trained as she was in classical Carnatic music. Dwarves and angels, talking doves, cloistered nuns, and traveling chefs featured in her stories and songs and the line between reality and fiction was often blurred. To this day, my sister Latha and I reminisce— *Remember that story, was that real?*

In *The Kerala Kitchen*, I have interspersed a variety of colorful stories among the recipes. Some of these tales come from my mother and others are my memories of journeys into the backwaters and plantations which gave birth to our family. Through them, I aspire to portray the cultural and culinary riches of this ancient community—the Syrian Christians of Kerala.

THE SYRIAN CHRISTIANS OF KERALA

A Brief History

The thriving town of Muchiri where the beautiful large ships of the Yavanas (Greeks), bringing gold, come splashing the white foam on the waters of the Periyar, which belongs to to the Cherala (Kings of Kerala) and return laden with pepper …

—Tamil poet Erakkadur Thyankannar

Long before the time of Christ, spice merchants and travelers from around the world would visit Kerala. The important seaport of Muziris or Cranganore was populated with Greeks, Syrians, Jews, and Chinese traders who lived in harmony with the people of the region. It was on one of these trading vessels, plying between Alexandria and the Malabar Coast, that Saint Thomas the Apostle is believed to have arrived in Cranganore in AD 52. He began preaching the Gospel to the people of these areas, and eventually established churches in Cranganore, Paravoor, Palur, Kokkamangalam, Niranam, Malayatoor, and Nillackel. Among those early conversions were several Namboodiri Brahmin families, from whom many of the present-day Syrian Christians trace their roots.

As legend has it, the upper caste Brahmins of Palur were converted after a miracle, whereby Mar Thoma (Saint Thomas) suspended water in midair as a testimony of his faith. Most of these early Christians followed the ancient Eastern Nestorian faith and were known as Malabar Christians until the advent of a Syrian merchant—Thomas of Canaan—who arrived in Muziris with four hundred Syrians, including several priests and a bishop. The Syrians were welcomed by the local Malabar Christians as the countrymen of Jesus and Saint Thomas. The two communities eventually intermarried and merged to become Syrian Christians, now recognized as one of the oldest Christian communities in the world.

The present-day Syrian Christians of Kerala are also known as Nazaranis, the followers of

Cheriapally, a 600-year-old church in Kottayam. (Inset) *The Syrian Christian Menorah*

Jesus of Nazareth, and though they are now divided broadly into four sects—the Knanaya Christians, Jacobites, Marthomites, and Syrian Catholics (Syro-Malabar Church)—they share many common religious and social practices, and intermarriage is not uncommon. Collectively they retain a distinct identity and remain independent from other Christians in India because of their unique lineage. Life is centered around their liturgy and the observance of days of fasting and abstinence. They follow old Syrian church rites, chanting in singsong Syriac liturgy. The saga of the St. Thomas Christians is narrated in their song and dance forms—*Margam Kali* (the way of St. Thomas) and the *Rabban Pattu* (the songs of Rabban).

Syrian Christians are identified by their family names which reflect the profession of a family elder, place of origin, or sometimes nothing but pure whimsy. My own family, a large Syrian Catholic clan from Kanjirapally, is called Pallivathukkal, meaning "at the church gate," as many centuries earlier my ancestors had settled near a church in Nillackel. My husband's family name, Thekkekunnel, means "south hill." Thadikaren, another family name, means "bearded man," and the poetic Myladi means "peacock dance." First names are biblical, and customarily the firstborn is named after a paternal grandparent and the secondborn after a maternal grandparent. Thereafter, aunts, uncles, and saints lend their names to the newborns. The second name is taken from the child's father, but a Joseph George, say, may be anonymous until, when paired with his family name, he can be immediately placed as Joseph, the son of George of the Pottenkulam family. Syrian Christian names are distinctive and a George may also be known as Varkey or Varghese; a Paul can be Peeli or Paulose; and an Abraham can be called Avira or Ittira. Similarly, the female Syrian Christian name Rachel may be Raahel; Elizabeth can be Aley or Elamma; and Bridget, the melodious Urshita.

Most prominent Syrian Christian families are close-knit and connected by an intricate web of marriages. I have vivid memories of my mother and sisters spending hours disentangling family connections, the links being the women who married into each family. With many of these large clans expanding into several hundred members, some families now hold periodic *kudumbayogams*, family get-togethers which allow members of the family to reconnect.

Christianity in India has long been synonymous with education and the Syrian Christians have made a significant contribution to this field, partly by means of the large number of clergy in the community. Today they have evolved into a distinct, indigenous community of agriculturists, scholars, industrialists, and professionals. A large number have moved to other cities in India as well as to distant lands, and though erudite and cosmopolitan, they are still attached to the traditions and customs of their ancestors.

Described as "Hindu in culture, Christian in religion, and Syro-Oriental in worship," Syrian Christians enjoy the status of a prosperous and socially prominent community.

The Church and Syrian Christians: Birth, Marriage, Death

The social life of orthodox Syrian Christians in Kerala revolves around the church and family, both firmly entwined. Every auspicious occasion—be it a marriage, death, housewarming, or business venture—is officiated in the presence of a family cleric. Many large families even today have at least one member of that vocation. Marriages, first communions, christenings, and other celebrations take place almost entirely within the larger family and community. Though many traditions and customs have been discarded and forgotten, the ancient rites of passage—birth, marriage, and death—are still observed with particular ceremony. The Knanaya Christians, descendants of the early Syriac-Jewish clans, have retained many old Jewish customs, such as the traditional bridal canopy and the custom of burying their dead facing the East.

There are many rituals associated with birth and the forty days that follow. In the last months of her pregnancy, the expectant mother is brought to her parent's home after a brief ceremony. Soon after the child is born, the newborn is given a pinch of gold and honey—symbolic of the riches, figurative or otherwise, that life holds for him. After childbirth, the ritual oil massages, baths, and other age-old customs are observed by most people even today.

Traditionally, Syrian Christian marriages are arranged by the family. A prospective groom or

bride is sought when a person reaches a marriageable age. The *streedhanam* (the "bride's share" or dowry) is discussed and often bargained over. The couple meet at a formal introduction called the *pennu kannal,* and if they are agreeable, the families negotiate and plan for the wedding. The *manasambandham* (engagement day) is celebrated with a mass and the bride and groom are pledged to one another in church. Auspicious days, Lent, and school holidays are all considered before a date is decided upon. The marriage ceremony is austere and unostentatious, the bride and groom customarily dressed in white. The exception to this sobriety is the large amount of gold worn by the bride. After the Christian ceremony, the groom ties onto his new wife a *thali mala* (the gold chain worn by married Indian women, a throwback to old Hindu customs), after which he also places the *manthrakodi* (the bridal sari) on the bride's shoulders; both gifts are then blessed by the priest. In the Knanaya community, the women now sing praises for the mother who has raised her daughter to be the fine young woman she is.

A death in the large and interconnected Syrian Christian community sees members of all related families paying their respects to the bereaved family. The immediate family mourns for forty days, the seventh day being observed with a mass for the deceased, followed by a communal breakfast. After the fortieth day, the soul of the departed is said to be released from earthly bonds, and the family parts after mass and the customary breakfast.

Bridegroom draping the **manthrakodi** *(wedding sari) over the bride's head*
(bride & groom: Marie George Kuruvinakunnel and Chacko Antony Ettukettil)

Syrian Christian woman in traditional attire

Traditional Attire

Customary attire for Syrian Christian men is a starched white *mundu* (rectangular piece of unstitched cloth, worn around the waist like a sarong) worn with a *jibba* (shirt). The traditional attire for women, though not embraced by the present generation, was a crisp white *mundu* with a fantail and a *chatta* (blouse), draped with a gauzy *kavanni* shawl that was finely embroidered or trimmed with gold *kasavu* brocade. Large gold *kunakku* hoops traditionally adorned the upper ears, while the lobes were fashionably stretched and elongated. Gold chains, bangles, and among the wealthier clans, an *arinjana mala* (a broad waist chain), and *padissaram* (anklets) were worn. Now the sari has replaced the *chatta* and *mundu*, and only the older matriarchs can be found wearing traditional clothes like these.

Days of Note

Christmas and Holy Week are observed through age-old rituals and the days preceding them are spent in fasting and prayer. On Maundy (Holy) Thursday, *kurisappam* (an unleavened bread) and *pesaha paal* (Passover milk) are prepared. After a supper of *kanji* (rice gruel) and *vanpayar* (red beans), a family elder reads a passage from the Bible, followed by prayers and hymns. The head of the family then breaks the *kurisappam*, dips it in the *pesaha paal* and shares it with the family in a symbolic reenactment of Jesus' Last Supper. This solemn ceremony has similarities to the Jewish Passover Seder, and it is believed that it was inherited from the early Syrian Jews, handed down over generations. Weddings and festive occasions are not held during the twenty-five days of Advent and the forty days of Lent.

In My Grandmother's House

The trip from Allepey to Kanjirapally took us most of the day, stopping at three ferry points—Palathuruthy, Nedumudi, and Kidangara. At each *kadathu* we got off, stretched our legs, and bought snacks from the little tea shops at the edge of the water— tiny sugar biscuits and lime drops for the children, strong coffee in small glasses and *neyappams* (jaggery cakes) for my parents and the driver. The ferry was invariably across the water, and we were thrilled to find it had just left. This gave my sister Latha and I time to explore. Everything around us was new and exciting, though we had made this journey many times on our annual trips from Bombay.

Shashi, my oldest sister, wore a bored expression and sipped a sweet soda from a glass bottle with a marble stopper. Chandy, my older brother, had his head in a book and refused to get out of the car. Kurien, my other brother, was as excited as we were, and ran down to the water, asking if he could jump in. Though not as remote as Kuttanad and Chambakulam, here too life was lived at the water's edge. Little children dived and splashed in the water while their mothers washed clothes or gutted fresh fish for the afternoon meal.

The ferry glided in, a massive raft tethered with thick ropes across two large barges. The ferrymen expertly guided it home, aligning it to fit the tracks on the shore. After being moored to coconut tree posts, large planks were placed between the boat and the shore, and the passengers slowly disembarked. A small country bus, two cars, and a bullock cart followed patiently. Then it was our turn to embark and our sturdy Ambassador car was driven aboard where it was secured with wooden wedges. When the ferry was full, the boatmen jumped into the large barges under the raft, untied the ropes, and steered the ferry away from the shore with soft, rhythmic chants—*ailo, ailiaio*. Latha and I stood with our father at the railing, sucking sour lime drops, each of our hands clasped tight in one of his as we floated across the emerald green waters.

Many hours later, we began the ascent to Kanjirapally, passing thickly forested slopes, verdant valleys, and little waterfalls. The forests gave way to rubber plantations and sleepy little hamlets. Finally, we were in the last stretch before the Pallivathukkal *tharavad*, our ancestral family home. The slow pace of the car allowed us glimpses of the other *tharavads*—Kokkapally, Karimpanal, Kunnath, Olakkamakkil—all branches of the larger Pallivathukkal family and brothers of my grandfather Chandykunju. My mother

Family portrait at my grandmother's house in Kanjirapally

pointed out each house as she related stories of its occupants. My father said nothing but his eyes lit up. The air was dense with the spicy fragrance of wood smoke, nutmeg, and pepper—an aroma that was for me synonymous with my childhood summers in Kanjira-pally. The car turned around a corner, past the large dovecote by the gate, and we were there.

The *tharavad* looked unchanged. Large and rambling, its simple, clean lines were typical of the older estate house. *Velliammachi*—my grandmother—lived here and was never alone, as she was always visited by one of her many children. My father, her fourth son, Rockichan, had moved to Bombay many years before to expand the newly started family rubber business. Now we would make this trip each summer to visit my father's family after a week at my mother's home in Allepey.

We were greeted at the door by my father's sister, Lucy *kutty*, who was visiting along with her children. Cousins from Coimbatore and Kottayam were also here, and the house bustled with life. My grandmother was resting, we were told on our way to her room across the large hall and past the chapel. The walls were hung with framed photographs of ancestors, among them my grandfather. His imposing aristocratic features and fierce moustache belied the gentle, scholarly man that he had been.

Silently mouthing the familiar names, we trooped into my grandmother's room and greeted her with folded hands—"*Easho mishiaku sthuthiayirikatte*" (Praise Jesus the Messiah), and she replied, "*Ippozhum, ennaikum*" (Now and always). My grandmother— Kunju Mariamma of Kodupadam—was no less impressive than her late husband. Clothed in the Syrian Christian *chatta* and *mundu*, she wore her smooth white hair scraped back into a bun at the nape of her neck. Large gold *kunakkus* adorned her ear-lobes. Very much the matriarch, she had a regal bearing and I was suddenly shy as she turned to hand me boiled sweets from the glass jar on her table.

Lunch was served in the large dining room with men and younger children eating first. Large dishes of soft red rice, platters of spicy fried beef, duck roast, and smaller dishes of fiery red fish curry and vegetables, jugs of buttermilk, and small bowls of pickles were served in two sets across the large table. On the sideboard were plates of cubed mango, sliced pineapple, and fresh bananas. My grandmother ate early with her sons and sons-in-law and then retired to her room. Latha and I preferred to eat with the women and wandered over later to the L-shaped room next to the dining room where my mother sat with the aunts and older cousins at a long trestle table. Here the conversation was lively. Recipes, news of marriages and deaths, and scandalous stories were swapped across the table.

The younger cousins with Latha and me in tow decided to go down to the creek at the bottom of the hill. Past my grandmother's rose garden, we stopped at the chambanga tree to pick a bagful of the rosy pink love apples, then we headed down the mossy, weathered steps. The rubber estate began here and we stopped again to watch the fresh white rubber sap dripping into the coconut shell receptacles. We picked bits of coagulated rubber from the old slashes and soon we were pelting one another with hard little rubber balls, shrieking and ducking behind trees and the lines of latex sheets hung up to dry by the old smokehouse. Verghese, the estate manager, walked over.

The previous year, my sister Latha had committed the unthinkable. Pointing to a rubber tree, she had asked what type of tree that was. Now, Verghese considered it his duty to educate each of us, the children of rubber planters, about the rudiments of running a rubber estate.

We were in the middle of the once-vast Pallivathukkal estate, now divided and sub-divided among its numerous progeny. The air was pungent with the cloying aroma of ripe jackfruit. The constant buzz of cicadas grew louder and in the distance we heard the trumpeting of an estate elephant. The trees thinned out and then, jumping over a stone stile, we were at the road by the creek. The water ran cold and swift, but was shallow enough for wading and collecting fish in our little glass jars.

Hours later, we returned to the house to find my mother and aunts still at the trestle table. There were cups of sweet tea on trays and tins of *palaharams* had been brought out from the storeroom. Sugary frosted *cheedas*, savory *kozhallappam* rolls, grainy cones of *churuttu*, and thick slices of syrupy pineapple jam roll were placed on white ceramic platters. Hot plantain fritters arrived from the kitchen, golden crisp on the outside and meltingly soft as you bit in.

More cousins arrived. They were the children of my father's older brother who lived on an estate nearby. Their mother would not be coming, the youngest announced. Everyone smiled when they heard that and I remembered why. Last summer, my aunt had gone to the rose garden and, seeing her husband seated on a garden bench, crept up behind him, flinging her arms around his shoulders. Then glancing down, she discovered it was not her husband, but my father who sat frozen in his seat. Horrified, she ran to tell my mother and, though it was all a joke now, I could understand why she had not come. I might have made the same mistake, I thought, since my father and his brother did look alike, both tall and broad shouldered.

After an early supper of *kanji*, *payar*, and leftovers from lunch, we moved into the small chapel next to the dining room. There were five pews on either side with prayer books and Bibles. Fresh hibiscus blooms in brass vases had been placed on the ornate wooden altar. On the wall were pictures of saints and a sepia photograph of my father's sister, Aley *kutty*, who had died young—of heartbreak, and we later learned, a fatal disease. She looked beautiful and tragic and I remembered her story, related many times over, of unrequited love and the events that followed—this is the stuff movies are made of, I thought passionately.

Velliammachi sat in the first pew, a large wooden rosary in hand, with the men on the benches behind her. Though there were enough seats, the women and children were scattered around on floor mats. The evening prayers began. After the full rosary, verses from the Bible were read out by one of the children, followed by prayers for the deceased. The prayers, chanted in singsong Syriac liturgy, were like soothing lullabies. Our bodies swayed, and our eyes drooped, as the familiar drone of ancient rhythms and the whiff of candlesmoke and frankincense enveloped us.

The next morning, Latha and I were up early drinking glasses of sweet black coffee with my father and uncles on the long, broad verandah that ran almost the length of the house. After breakfast, we planned to visit the grassy flat where the old elephant was kept many years ago. My cousin Rosie, the leader of our little group, led the way, as she lived in nearby Kottayam and was knowledgeable about events in this part of the world. Stopping at the mango tree, we plucked small, sweet mangoes from the lower branches. The tree was heavy with fruit and soon our arms were full. Down at the clearing, we stopped at the large stone basin which once held the gruel for the elephant. Nearby, a large hook attached to a stake still held the iron fetters and chains that would restrain the elephant. They had been forced to shoot Kuttan the elephant years earlier and though we had heard the story many times before, we begged Rosie to relate the gory tale once more.

Rosie was a good storyteller, pausing dramatically at just the right places, her large, expressive eyes round with emotion. Many years ago, she began, before any of us were born, Kuttan the elephant had been kept here to transport timber and haul other produce around the estate. Paapu was the old mahout who took care of the elephant and the two of them would often be seen deep in conversation as if they had a secret language. One day at feeding time, Paapu was preparing hot gruel in the huge vat over the wood fire. He had many helpers but always insisted on supervising the meal preparation himself, making sure that the gruel was cooked just the way Kuttan loved it. On this particular day everything had gone wrong; the gruel was late in cooking, and the hungry elephant was stamping his foot impatiently. In their haste, the helpers inadvertently poured the hot gruel onto the irritable elephant's foot. The angry animal roared with pain and reared, bringing his huge foot down onto Paapu's head. The old mahout was crushed to death, Rosie concluded dramatically. *Crushed!*

"Why," I asked, breaking the hushed silence, "why did Kuttan kill the mahout he loved so much?"

Walking back to the house, the mood was somber. In the courtyard by the small dining room, my grandmother lay on a straw mat, covered only with a thin cloth, her smooth skin caked with a thick paste of mud. Her eyes were shaded and she did not see us. She has her mudbaths every Tuesday, Cousin Rosie whispered, and cannot be disturbed. Later, the herb-infused water that was boiling in the huge iron cauldron outside the bathing room would be used to wash off the medicated mud that coated her skin.

At eight, I was a precocious and imaginative child. Absorbing everything I saw around me, I tucked away memories and tales to relate to my friends in Bombay. How do I explain this, I wondered: a tragically dead aunt and an elephant on the rampage made exotic stories, but a scantily clad grandmother caked with mud?

The days passed quickly, and the rest of our stay was a blur of visits to the nearby *tharavads*—a wedding, a christening, a funeral, and a trip to the family graves, where a baby sister lay buried. It must be better I imagined— if you had to be dead— to be in the company of such a large family. Reading the many familiar names engraved on the marble grave-stones, it was comforting to know she was not alone. Death had been a frequent visitor to this large, entangled family.

THE TRADITIONAL
KERALA KITCHEN

The traditional kitchen can still be found in larger homes, estate bungalows, and some of the humbler farmhouses in Kerala. It centers around the hearth which has four to six *adupu* or stoves. The heat of each stove is controlled by the amount of wood placed in the fire—a steady flame for the *kanji* that simmers in the large pot, a vigorous fire for the swiftly prepared shrimp *olathiathu*, a slow-burning flame for the fish curry that will need to simmer in a *meen chatti* for its flavor to really catch, the glowing embers of the smallest *adupu* from which a few live coals may be lifted to place on the lid of the *appa chatti* (rice pancake griddle). Herbs, salted meat, and fish are hung to dry over the hearth and a jar of gooseberries may be left to smoke for days by the back burner.

The rest of the kitchen is spare and functional. Chopping and food preparation is accomplished on the kitchen table, using little wood-handled knives for vegetables and the larger cleaver for meat and seafood. Equally important is the little stone mortar and pestle in which small amounts of spices or chillis are crushed or powdered.

The kitchen countertop holds the grinding stone on which most of the daily spices are ground or crushed. This countertop also contains several large blocks of wood on which meat and fish are chopped. Oil and some spices for daily use are also kept here, having been measured out from the storeroom.

A deep stone sink can be found in a smaller room nearby and here the large pots and pans are scrubbed after cooking. The clean vessels are dried in the sun and then stored under the counter on open shelves. Daily cooking vessels include the *kalam*, for cooking rice; a few clay *mannu chattis* for fish curry and vegetables; the round-bottomed *cheena chatti* for roasting eggs; and the heavy bell-metal *urali* for meat roasts and *olathus*. There is also the *appa chatti* for lacy rice pancakes, the *puttu kuti* for steamed rice cakes, and the *chembu* for steaming plantains and rice cakes.

The storeroom, usually adjacent to the kitchen, is where large reserves of food staples and produce from the land are kept—bottles of spices and herbs, tins of rice flour and *palahaarams*, jars of coccum, salted mangoes, coconut oil, and a barrel of coarse sea salt. Large bunches of small *poovan* bananas and larger cooking plantains hang from hooks to ripen. During season, mangoes are also kept here in straw to ripen. Rice is traditionally stored in large earthenware pots or in a stout wooden granary box. From this room, the Syrian Christian housewife runs her home, measuring and handing out the ingredients needed for the day.

Larger homes have separate rooms for various functions—one for the storage of coconuts, vegetables, and other produce from the estate or farm; the wood room where dry wood is stored for the monsoons; and the *nellu ara* (granary), sometimes a large wooden room within a room, or a larger, double-storied structure. The *orapera* is another room set off of the main kitchen, where large amounts of rice flour, halvahs, and *palahaarams* are prepared. The hearth here is wider to accommodate massive vessels; some of these bell-metal pots are more than five feet wide and weigh more than a hundred pounds.

Many traditional kitchens continue to function in the above manner even today, with a smaller, modern kitchen close to the main kitchen, housing conveniences such as a gas stove, an electric grinder for spices and powders, a microwave oven, and a coffeemaker. But it is in the traditional, older kitchen that red country rice cooks in a *kalam*, a *chatti* of coccum-soured fish curry simmers, and an *urali* of spiced beef is slowly stirred and fried, absorbing the unmistakable flavor of woodsmoke.

Methods of Cooking and Vessels to Match

Puzhangiathu Boiled or steamed. A *chembu* is invaluable as a cooking vessel for steaming. It is traditionally made of copper or brass, though aluminum is now more frequently used. The *puttu kuti*, which is used for steaming *puttu*, has a round base pot in which water is boiled, and a tall cylindrical tube above this base in which rice flour and coconut are layered and steamed. (*Puttu*, Steamed Rice Cakes, page 37)

Olathiathu Sautéed in a *cheena chatti* which literally means "Chinese pot." This is a round-bottomed vessel with two handles, similar to a wok. The round bottom spreads the heat evenly through the base and into the food, which makes it ideal for sautéing and deep-frying. (*Mutta Roast*, Egg Roast, page 140)

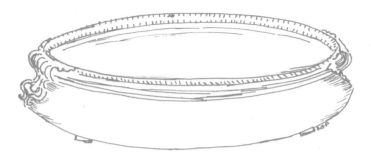

Chuttathu Steam cooked in an *appam chatti*. This is a heavy iron round-bottomed vessel with a lid, similar to the *cheena chatti*. The term also describes coal roasted (often used to prepare *Chakka Kuru*, jackfruit seeds). (*Paalappam*, Lace-rimmed Pancakes, page 40)

Purattiathu Mashed and seasoned in a *kalam*, a large rice vessel in which water, tapioca, or rice is boiled. (*Kappa Purattiathu*, Mashed and Seasoned Tapioca, page 57)

Pattichu olathiathu Dry-cooked with spices and stir-fried in an *urali*. This is a wide-mouthed, squat vessel made of bell metal, which gradually warms up and retains heat for a long time. It has a multitude of uses—to fry and roast meats, to cook halvahs, and to dry-roast rice flour. *Vaarpu*, larger vessels of this type, have two handles that are lifted with stout poles. (*Erachi Olathiathu*, Fried Meat, page 106)

Varathathu Deep-fried or sautéed, usually in a *cheena chatti*. (*Meen Varathathu*, Fried Fish, page 77)

Pattichu Varathathu Parboiled and fried, usually in an *urali*. (*Tharavu* Roast, Duck Roast, page 137)

Kachiyathu Warmed in a *cheena chatti*. (*Moru Kachiyathu*, Spiced Cooked Buttermilk, page 146)

Vevichathu Simmered in spices in a *meen chatti*—a round bottomed earthenware pot. (*Meen Vevichathu*, Fish Curry, Country-Style, page 87)

Pollichathu Broiled or roasted in an *urali*. (*Meen Pollichathu*, Fish Roasted in Banana Leaves, page 80)

Villachayathu Slowly stir-cooked in an *urali*. (*Black Halvah*, page 181)

Maavu Kuzhachathu Dough cooked to a soft ball in an *urali*. (*Idiappam*, Stringhoppers, page 35)

Roasting Slow-cooked in a heavy vessel like an *urali*, with coals placed on the lid, which creates a dry oven within the vessel. (*Panniyerachi Roast*, Pork Roast, page 118)

Kadugu Pottikinnu Bursting of mustard seeds in heated oil with whole red chillis; the resulting seasoned oil is poured into curries or vegetable dishes. This can be done in a small *cheena chatti*.

SYRIAN CHRISTIAN CUISINE

Like all large, multi-ethnic countries, India has a host of diverse foods, the cuisine of each region defined by the indigenous produce of the land and the various cultures that have influenced it. The cooking traditions of the Syrian Christians of Kerala show the influence of Arab, Chinese, Malay, Dutch, Portuguese, and Syrian cultures, along with ancient Hindu cooking practices.

Food is either simmered over a wood fire, quickly stir-fried, or sautéed, steamed, or roasted. According to statistics, 80 percent of the state still uses firewood for cooking, not entirely, I suspect, due to the shortage of alternative fuel options.

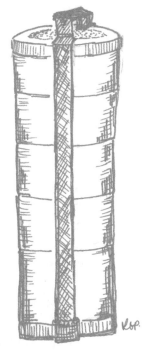

The diet is predominantly non-vegetarian, with much enthusiasm for seafood which is plentiful in this water world. Even the humblest home can be assured of a handful of sardines or tiny shrimps to carry a meal. Chicken, eggs, and beef are consumed often, whereas pork and duck are reserved for weddings and festive occasions. Vegetables are simply prepared with a few spices and steamed in their own juices, or simmered in yogurt and coconut. Rice is the staple food of the state, and red country rice is cooked over wood fires, to be eaten as *Kanji* (Rice Gruel) or as the base of every main meal. It is also powdered or ground to make a variety of steamed delicacies. Coconut in its various forms—fresh, ground, roasted, or as coconut milk—is used in most recipes. Coconut oil, the preferred cooking medium, complements and adds to the unique flavor of Malayali cuisine. Other key ingredients in traditional fare are tapioca, plantain, breadfruit, mango, coccum (a kind of tamarind), spices, curry leaves, shallots, and jaggery or *sarkara* (raw cane sugar).

Though authentic Syrian Christian food owes much of its flavor to the smoky embers of wood fires, fresh produce, and the special quality of stone-ground spices seasoned in traditional cooking vessels, modern alternatives can

19

be used with equal success. The heavy bell-metal *urali* can be replaced by the ubiquitous iron skillet, the rounded-bottomed *cheena chatti* by a wok, and any type of steamer can be used for the various steamed preparations. Today, the pressure cooker has become an invaluable cooking vessel for meats and fresh lentils and beans. Likewise, foil and plastic wrap can be used if banana leaves are un-available.

Yeast and fermented coconut water are good replacements for toddy, brown sugar can be used if jaggery is unavailable, and packaged spice powders and mill-ground rice flour work just fine. Though nothing can compare with the sweetness of fresh coconut, desiccated coconut or packaged coconut milk and powders are adequate replacements. Do not substitute coccum with sweet tamarind, instead use slices of tart green mango. As for that typically Malayali ingredient, coconut oil, I have specified its use only if the recipe demands it. Any other vegetable oil can be substituted. However, I do recommend a drizzle of virgin coconut oil if you want to experience the true flavor of Syrian Christian cuisine.

Menu for a Day

A day in a traditional Syrian Christian home starts with a steaming glass of black coffee sweetened with *sarkara* (raw cane sugar). Several glasses later, breakfast may consist of *Puttu* (Steamed Rice Cakes) served with *Kadala Karri* (Spicy Curried Chickpeas). Also on the table would be a platter of *Erachi Olathiathu* (Fried Beef) and *Meen Vevichathu* (Fish Curry cooked in a clay pot), both leftovers from the previous day. Steamed plantain halves in their skins are served hot and a bowl of fresh grated coconut is served on the side with *paani* (sweet palm syrup). Break-fast is rounded out with a plate of tiny *poovan* bananas and more coffee, this time frothy with a lib-eral dose of milk.

A mid-morning snack would consist of a bowl of *Kanji* or *Kappa* (Boiled Tapioca) and a dol-lop of fresh *Chamandi* (Chutney) accompanied by glasses of *Moru* (Spiced Cooked Buttermilk) or tender coconut water.

Lunch is invariably served late in the afternoon and features an array of dishes: boiled red country rice, *Erachi Olathiathu*, *Meen Vevichathu*, crisp fried fish, *thorans* (side dishes) of different vegetables, and again, spiced buttermilk. Pickles and chutney are also served. The meal ends with fresh fruit, yogurt, and *paani*.

Tea or coffee is served at around 5 p.m. with *palaharams* from the storeroom, and hot fried *Ethakka Appams* (Plantain Fritters) or *Kozhukotta* (Stuffed Rice Cakes).

Dinner is usually light, very often *Kanji* and *Cherupayar* (Mung Beans) with a fresh chutney, pickles, and *pappadams* (flatbreads made from lentil flour). Leftovers from lunch are also placed on the table, and a spicy omelet is rustled up if needed.

SPICES AND HERBS OF KERALA

Throughout history, the lure of spices has led the adventurous to unexplored lands. Spices have been a driving force, creating new empires which have in turn birthed new religions and cultures. Much of the world's spices come from India—and Kerala produces most of these spices. The mountainous eastern region of Kerala has the perfect climate to support pepper, nutmeg, cardamom, cinnamon, cloves, and turmeric. Kerala's spice trade dates back three thousand years to when the world's first spice traders, the Phoenicians and Arabs, took spices to Rome and Greece. Even today, Kerala retains its importance as a major producer in the world's spice trade.

Spices and herbs are used to improve and enhance the flavor of food, their piquant taste and aroma adding a delicious touch to sauces, marinades, and gravies. They also have nutritional value, as they are rich in calcium, iron, vitamins, and antioxidants. Most herbs and spices have medicinal properties and are used in the preparation of simple home remedies and ayurvedic medicines.

Spices can be used whole, powdered, fried, roasted, or as a curry paste. They are used in the various stages of cooking, on their own, or like a magic formula in combination with other spices. To the novice, the use of spices may seem bewildering at first, but once you know your spices and the different flavors and aromas they release when heated, the rest is easy. A curry can be toned down or spiced up by adjusting the amount of spices you add to it. Most spices need to be lightly heated—roasted, fried, or steamed—to remove their raw smell and to release their flavor. For this reason, it is essential to add them at the precise time in the cooking process. Seasoning is the subtle finale to a lightly spiced curry or vegetable dish—the addition of oil seasoned with mustard seeds and curry leaves imparts a burst of flavor to a simply prepared dish.

In traditional Kerala recipes, herbs and spices are freshly ground on a grinding stone in different combinations and textures—a thick paste of coriander, turmeric, chilli powder, and black pepper for a spicy chicken curry; a pounded paste of red chillis, turmeric, ginger, and garlic for a piquant fish curry; a coarse crush of coconut, green chilli, and turmeric to prepare a vegetable *thoran*.

Whole spices can be powdered in a coffee grinder and stored in airtight containers for convenience. In this form, they can be quickly tossed into a small blender to make a curry paste or used directly as powders. Spices are also available as powders either on their own or as packaged mixes such as your average supermarket chicken curry mix or vegetable curry mix—*not* recommended for the discerning cook!

When I first started cooking, I would question the necessity of certain herbs and spices and would decide to do without them, often discovering later that the small but vital ingredient actually made the dish. Certain spices can be difficult to appreciate at first appraisal, like the

21

medicinal-tasting turmeric, which few Indian dishes can do without, or the innocuous-looking curry leaf that graces many a South Indian curry. Asafoetida was, in particular, my pet peeve, and early on I decided to banish the offending spice from my kitchen. Years later, watching a Western cooking show on TV, *Cooking with Kurma*, I was amazed to discover the chef's passion for the bitter, foul-smelling spice. He could never have enough of it, often adding the magic ingredient to soups and pastas. Wondering what the fuss was about, I decided to experiment and was instantly converted. Recently, when complimented on a well-prepared dish, I was asked what the secret ingredient was and I replied smugly, "asafoetida, of course."

Though most spices and herbs are available in Indian food stores and markets, herbs such as coriander, fenugreek, mustard, mint, and curry leaf can be cultivated in pots or herb gardens for their aromatic leaves. As a landscape designer, I try to fit an herb garden into many of the gardens I design. In my own herb garden, seven thousand feet above sea level in the Palani Hills, South India, Western cooking herbs such as rosemary and peppermint rub leaves with Indian medicinal herbs such as *vellarai* (an anticarcinogenic herb), *brahmi* (a herb that improves memory), and *marikolandu* (a herb that prevents nightmares). I haven't had much success with my curry leaf plant, transported from Kerala. It can grow into a thirty-foot tree in warmer climes but is a spindly shrub here in my own backyard.

Last year on a blustery October afternoon when I was visiting the Bronx's Wave Hill, a public garden in New York City, I was delighted to find an old-fashioned herb garden planted with spices and herbs from all parts of the world. There in a corner of the walled enclosure was a fine specimen of the *muraya koenigii*—the humble curry leaf tree from India.

Commonly used Spices and Herbs of Kerala Cuisine

Asafoetida *Khayam (Ferula asafetida)*
In Latin, *asa* means "resin," *foetidus* is "fetid" or "foul smelling."
Botanical Source: This spice comes from the resin of the asafoetida plant, a member of the carrot family.
Available Forms: Asafoetida is available as a resinous nugget, or as a powder mixed with rice flour to make it easier to use.
Medicinal Use: Asafoetida is used for its digestive properties and for relief from flatulence.
Culinary Use: Strongly flavored, bitter, and indeed almost foul-smelling, the spice should be used sparingly. As is the case with most spices, heat pleasantly enhances its flavor. Asafoetida is used in a variety of South Indian food preparations that are transformed by a pinch of the spice.
Example: Tomato Chutney/*Thakali Chamandhi*, page 148

Cardamom *Elakka* (*Elettaria cardamomumi*)

Cardamom is a widely used aromatic spice, valued the world over for its medicinal properties as well as culinary uses.

Botanical Source: Pods are harvested from a perennial bush when ripe and then sun-dried.

Available Forms: Sun-dried cardamom pods can be used whole or freshly ground; also available ground.

Medicinal Use: Cardamom is used as a digestive aid and stimulant.

Culinary Use: Cardamom has a warm, seductive flavor and aroma. It is an important ingredient in Indian cuisine and is used in a variety of food preparations, both sweet and savory.

Example: Plantain and Coconut Sauté/*Ethakka Vilayachathu*, page 177

Chilli Peppers *Molagu* (*Capsicum frutescens*)

Chillis come in many shapes and sizes and in varying degrees of pungency.

Botanical Source: Chilli peppers belong to the nightshade family that includes bell peppers, tomatoes, and eggplants. The *Capsicum frutescens*, a long, slim chilli pepper, is the variety used most frequently in Indian cooking.

Available Forms: Fresh, green; sun-dried, red; whole or as chilli powder.

Culinary Use: Chilli peppers can be mildly spicy to fiery hot, and the color may vary from green when fresh to orange-red to a dark red when dried. Though virtually odorless, they have a strong, pungent flavor that complements the food they are cooked with. Chilli pepper is one of the principal spices in Indian cuisine, and is used as a whole spice for seasoning, or alternately, powdered, crushed, or ground into a paste.

Example: Fish Curry, Country-Style/*Meen Vevichathu*, page 87

Cinnamon *Patta* (*Cinnamomum Verum*)

Once valued more than gold, cinnamon has over the ages been associated with rituals of sacrifice and pleasure. Different cultures have sought it for a multitude of uses—embalming, witchcraft, religious rites, and as an invaluable cooking ingredient in many world cuisines. It grew to be the most profitable of spices in the spice trade.

Botanical Source: Harvested from the bushy evergreen cinnamomum tree, the bark of the tree is scraped, rolled into cylinders, and dried in indirect sunlight.

Available Forms: Cinnamon sticks; ground

Culinary Use: The flavor and aroma of cinnamon is sweet and warm. It is used extensively in baked items, both sweet and savory, and is one of the ingredients in the versatile spice mix garam masala, used extensively in Indian cooking.

Example: Chicken Stew/*Kozhi Ishtew*, page 127

Clove *Grambu* (*Syzigium aromaticum*)

A small, nail-shaped spice, clove derives its name from the French word *clou*, meaning "nail." It is indigenous to the island of Malacca in Indonesia, where natives are known to wear a necklace of cloves to ward off evil spirits and illness. The Dutch tried to monopolize the clove trade by eradicating cloves on all but two islands in Indonesia, but the French broke this monopoly by smuggling cloves from India to the rest of the world. Today, Zanzibar, in Tanzania, is the world's largest producer of cloves.

Botanical Source: Harvested from the tropical evergreen tree *Syzigium aromaticum*, the plant's tender buds are dried in the sun for days.

Available Forms: Whole; ground

Medicinal Use: Clove has antiseptic properties and is used as a local anesthetic for toothaches, in addition to treating flatulence, colic, indigestion, and nausea.

Spices at a Kerala market

Culinary Use: Clove has a strong, medicinal aroma and flavor. An important ingredient in Indian cooking, it is one of the spices used in garam masala and curry mixes. As its etymology implies, cloves are often studded into roasts and used to secure leaf parcels of food. They are also used in pickles, stews, and preserves.
Example: Pork Roast/*Panniyerachi* Roast, page 118

Coccum *Kodam puli* (*Garcinia indica*)
Botanical Source: Coccum is the little-known fruit of the evergreen Garcinia tree, found in the rainforests of the Western Ghats of India. After the fruit is harvested, the thick outer rind is sun-dried till it turns dark and shrivels. It can then be stored for years and used when needed.
Available Form: Dried
Medicinal Use: Coccum is used to treat tumors and heart complaints. It has also been used for its weight-reducing properties.
Culinary Use: Almost odorless, coccum is faintly sweet and extremely sour, with a unique smoky flavor. Prized by Malayalis for its distinct flavor, coccum is used in most seafood preparations in Kerala.
Example: Shrimp in Ground Coconut Curry/*Thenga Arache Chemmeen Karri*, page 98

Coriander *Malli* (*Coriandrum sativum*)
One of the oldest recorded spices, coriander has been mentioned in ancient Sanskrit texts and in the Bible, and has even been found in the tombs of pharaohs.
Botanical Source: Coriander is the tiny berry from an annual plant of the parsley family. Coriander seeds are harvested from the mature plant. The fresh leaves are called cilantro, and also used for cooking.
Available Forms: Whole seeds; ground; fresh leaves
Medicinal Use: Coriander has antispasmodic and carminative properties. Considered an aphrodisiac, its seeds were once used in love potions. The spice is also used in herbal oils and medicines.
Culinary Use: Both coriander and cilantro are aromatic and strongly flavored. Coriander seeds, powdered or whole, are used in curries; the leaves are used for chutneys, curries, and as a garnishing.
Example: Kerala Chicken Curry/*Kozhi Karri*, page 126

Cumin *Jeeragam* (*Cuminum cyminum*)

In ancient times, cumin symbolized greed and avarice, but through the ages it came to represent faithfulness.

Botanical Source: The cumin seed is harvested from an annual plant in the parsley family.

Available Forms: Whole seeds; powder

Medicinal Use: Cumin has antispasmodic, sedative, and antibacterial properties.

Culinary Use: Like most spices, cumin has an aromatic and spicy flavor, intensifying in taste when heated. Cumin is used with other spices in curries and in seasoning oil.

Example: Spinach with Crushed Coconut/*Cheera Thoran*, page 52

Curry Leaf *Karivepala* (*Murraya koenigii*)

Curry leaf is not to be confused with the ground spice mixture known as curry.

Botanical Source: The curry leaf is harvested from the curry leaf plant, a perennial tropical shrub of the citrus family.

Available Form: Leaves

Culinary Use: Curry leaf has a mild aroma and flavor, which is enhanced further when heated in oil. Used fresh, it can be stored for weeks if kept refrigerated. Curry leaf is used in seasoning oil with mustard seeds and other accompaniments, and in curries, chutneys, and vegetable dishes. It is an essential ingredient in rendering the authentic flavor of South Indian and in particular, Kerala cuisine.

Example: Curried Chickpeas/*Kadala Karri*, page 71

Fenugreek *Uluva* (*Trigonella foenum*)

Botanical Source: Fenugreek is obtained from an annual herb of the pea family. The seeds are harvested from the mature plant and dried.

Available Forms: Leaves; seeds

Medicinal Use: Fenugreek has many medicinal properties, and is valued for its high iron content. It has been known to be a cure for baldness, diabetes, high blood pressure, and anemia. It is also used as a digestive aid and to improve lactation in women and cows.

Culinary Use: The flavor of fenugreek is bitter, strong, and faintly sweet. In Kerala cuisine, the seeds are used in curry powders, in seasonings, and as a flavoring and thickener in curries and pickles. The leaves, popular in North Indian cuisine, can be freshly sauteed or dried to add flavor to curries.

Example: Fish Pickle/*Meen Achaar*, page 202

Garlic *Vellutha ulli* (*Allium sativum*)

Garlic features in the mythology, religion, and culture of many countries over the ages. According to Arab legend, garlic grew from the devil's footprints as he left the garden of Eden. The Bible mentions garlic as one of the foods the Hebrews enjoyed during their sojourn in Egypt. In Europe, garlic has been widely used in cooking since the days of the Roman Empire, and has also been used to ward off vampires and evil spirits.

Botanical Source: Garlic belongs to the lily plant family, and has subterranean bulbs divided into numerous cloves. The garlic bulb is sun-dried after harvesting.

Available Forms: Fresh in a bulb that can be separated into cloves; fresh cloves can be chopped, sliced, or made into a paste; also sold in stores as a powder.

Medicinal Use: Garlic has many medicinal properties. Regular consumption of garlic has been known to reduce blood pressure and cholesterol levels. It aids digestion and prevents flatulence. It is also helpful in the treatment of diabetes, and is used in home remedies for coughs and colds.

Culinary Use: The flavor of raw garlic is strong and pungent. Once cooked, it has an intense but pleasant flavor and aroma. Garlic is an important ingredient in Indian cuisine. In Kerala, garlic is used in many forms as the recipe demands—whole, sliced, crushed, or ground to a paste. It blends well with onion, ginger, and chillis to form a thick base for curries.
Example: Yesterday's Fish Curry/*Meen Vevichathu*, page 86

Ginger *Ingi* (*Zingiber officionale*)
Ginger is traditionally held to be a spice with universal appeal. Like garlic, it appears through history in many cultures. It is believed to have originated in India, though early travelers have carried the root to every corner of the earth.
Botanical Source: Ginger is harvested from the rhizomes of the zingibera plant which are cleaned and dried in the sun.
Available Forms: Fresh root; paste; ground to a powder; preserved in sweet syrup; pickled
Medicinal Use: Ginger has several medicinal properties and is used in home remedies as well as ayurvedic and allopathic medicines. It is known to be beneficial in the treatment of nausea, chest congestion, colds, coughs, asthma, colic, rheumatism, and loss of appetite. Like garlic, it also lowers blood pressure and cholesterol levels.
Culinary Use: Mildly aromatic, fresh ginger has a pleasantly pungent flavor. It is used in a variety of sweet and savory food preparations, and is one of the principal ingredients in Kerala cuisine. It should be peeled before using.
Example: Sweet-and-Sour Ginger Curry/*Inji Puli*, page 65

Mustard *Kadugu* (*Brassica juncea*)
Mustard seed is an indispensable ingredient in world cuisine. Its versatility has made this tiny seed the most widely used spice, in terms of sheer volume.
Botanical Source: The seeds are obtained from the seed pods of mustard plants.
Available Forms: Whole seeds; powder; a paste blended with vinegar and other ingredients to tone down its sharpness
Medicinal Use: Mustard paste is used in poultices as a cure for chest colds. It is also used as a laxative and an emetic, and to relieve rheumatic and muscular aches and pains.
Culinary Use: Mustard seeds produce a strong, pungent oil that is used in some ethnic cuisines. Though practically odorless, it compensates with a flavor that is intense and pungent which complements the food it is teamed with. In Kerala, mustard seeds are ground to a paste in certain dishes, but more often are used as a seasoning in hot oil. The fresh leaves of the mustard plant are consumed as greens, and the oil from the seeds is also used in curries.
Example: Mixed Vegetable Curry/*Avial*, page 54

Nutmeg *Jadhikka* (*Myristica fragrans*)
Nutmeg has been traded on the spice route since early times and is one of the most versatile of spices.
Botanical Source: The nutmeg is obtained from the fruit of the evergreen *myristica* tree indigenous to Southeast Asia. The tree yields fruit about eight years after planted and continues to bear fruit for sixty years or more. Once harvested, the ripe fruit that encases the hard brown nut is removed, and the lacy red covering known as mace is separated and dried. (Mace has a more delicate flavor and fragrance.) The nutmeg seed is then dried until it rattles in its shell.
Available Forms: Whole (to be freshly grated); ground (mace is usually ground.)

Nutmeg and mace drying in the sun

Medicinal Use: Nutmeg oil is used in the treatment of rheumatic pain and toothaches.

Culinary Use: An important ingredient in both Western and Eastern cuisine, nutmeg is used in curries, baked products, and beverages. Ground or powdered nutmeg is an important flavoring ingredient in Kerala sweets and savories.

Example: Rosa Cookies/*Achappam*, page 164

Pepper *Kurumolagu* (*Piper nigrum*)

Pepper in its various forms is one of the most widely used spices in the world. This is the spice that took early spice traders to Kerala, from where it was transported to the rest of the world.

Botanical Source: Peppercorns are the berries of the *Piper nigrum*, a perennial climber that is indigenous to the Malabar Coast. The ripe berries are picked when they turn red and then scalded in boiling water so they turn black. They are then dried in the sun for days. White pepper, milder in flavor, is obtained by removing the outer pericarp of the softened berries, then submerging them in water for weeks and later sun-drying them. Green pepper is the immature berry of the same plant, and it has a crunchy, pungent taste. Black pepper is the most pungent, both in flavor and aroma.

Available Forms: Black and white pepper are sold whole or ground; green pepper is often found pickled in brine.

Medicinal Use: Pepper is often used in home remedies for colds, coughs, and nausea.

Culinary Use: An important ingredient in Kerala cooking, pepper is used ground or whole in a variety of dishes.

Example: Mutton Pepper Fry/*Atterachiyum Kurumolagu Olathiathu*, page 116

Tamarind *Vaalam puli* (*Tamarindus indicia*)

The tamarind, a native of East Africa, is now grown extensively in India, and the name literally means "date of India."

Botanical Source: Fresh tamarind is a plump brown pod, with a thick, paste-like pulp that contains large seeds.

Available Forms: Whole fruit; ground; paste

Medicinal Use: Tamarind is used as a laxative and also as a digestive.

Culinary Use: Tamarind has a faintly sour odor, and a sweet-and-sour flavor. It is used, along with other spices, in a variety of curries and chutneys.

Example: Shallots with Tamarind and Roasted Coconut/*Thiyal*, page 61

Turmeric *Manjal* (*Curcuma longa*)

Turmeric is one of the most ancient and valued spices in India, though its use did not spread to the rest of the world until recent times.

Botanical Source: The turmeric plant is a herbaceous perennial with dense clumps of subterranean rhizomes. After harvesting, the clumps are removed and cleaned. They are cured by first boiling in water, and then dried in the sun until they are hard and dry.

Available Forms: Whole dry bulbs; bright yellow powder

Medicinal Use: Turmeric has many medicinal properties. It is known to be a natural antiseptic and blood purifier, as well as a potent antioxidant. It is invaluable in its use as a simple home remedy for diarrhea and other stomach ailments. Ground into a paste with sandalwood powder, its antiseptic and healing properties prevent and cure acne and sunburn.

Culinary Use: Turmeric has a faintly medicinal flavor and aroma. An important ingredient in Indian cooking, it is used along with other spices for curries and other dishes.

Example: Spiced Cooked Buttermilk/*Moru Kachiyathu*, page 146

Preparation of Spices

Though they are traditionally ground on a grinding stone, spices can be prepared with equal success by using electrical tools. They can be ground to a fine paste in the small jar of a blender, or alternately, powdered or crushed in a coffee grinder that is used solely for spices. Spices and herbs can be coarsely crushed by processing in short bursts, or ground to a smooth paste by processing for a longer period.

Standard Curry Preparation

Frying the Spices: In a standard curry preparation, the oil is heated in a heavy-bottomed vessel over low heat. The onions are added and fried until soft (about 1 minute), or translucent (1½ minutes), light brown (2 to 3 minutes), or a darker brown (3 to 5 minutes) as specified in the recipe. The ginger and garlic are added and the frying is continued until the mixture is soft or brown, each addition taking a minute or longer.

Next come the spices; this is the crucial stage, and it determines the fate of your curry. If you rush this, the curry will have a raw unsavory flavor and if the heat is turned up too high, you may end up burning your spices. As one cooking instructor once put it, "use your three senses—your ears to hear the sizzle, your eyes to see it happen, and your nose, the most important of all, to sense the moment." To fry the *arapu* (spice mixture) add the spices at various stages as specified in the recipe. Stir continuously through the entire process to prevent the spices from sticking to your pan. The spices release their aromatic oils and fragrances as they are heated, and settle at the bottom of your pan, allowing the oil to rise and signal to you that they are ready.

In the next stage, you can add the fish, meat, or vegetable as the recipe specifies, and later the water or coconut milk.

Coconut: Fruit of the Tree of Life

He who plants a coconut tree, plants food and drink, vessels and clothing,
a home for himself, and a heritage for his children.

—South Seas saying

The truth of this saying is evident in Kerala, where the swaying fronds of the coconut palm dot the landscape of this lush and bountiful land. It is rare to find a household, however humble, that does not have at least a couple of coconut palms in its backyard. The coconut tree is generous in its myriad uses—its wood for timber, its fronds for thatching roofs, the coconut husk to be spun into coir for ropes and carpets. The list is endless. Culturally, the coconut is auspicious and symbolizes prosperity. Used in religious ceremonies, at weddings, and to celebrate new ventures, a coconut even takes the place of the champagne bottle, smashed against the hull of a new ship in celebration.

The fruit is nourishing and a delicious base for a host of food preparations. Malayalis cherish the coconut and scoff at any talk of cholesterol and other health problems that may be caused by coconuts. Indeed, no other cuisine has such a comprehensive range of coconut-based dishes. And there is good news for coconut lovers—this is the year of the coconut, as skinny models and health gurus now swear by its beneficial properties.

The water of the tender coconut, besides being a refreshing drink, has medicinal properties for heart, liver, and kidney disorders. Recent reports state that tender coconut water has been known to reduce the viral load of HIV.

The water of the mature coconut is an excellent isotonic electrolyte, and the flesh is a source of sugar, fiber, proteins, antioxidants, vitamins, and minerals. There are even reports of coconut water being used during war-time as an intravenous fluid to save lives. The firm flesh is grated or ground and the milk extracted for curries, sweets, and savories. The dried flesh produces copra and coconut oil, the favorite cooking oil of Kerala. Toddy, also known as *kallu*—the fermented sap tapped from the trunk of the tree—is a sweet local brew that is available in toddy shops all over the state. Fresh toddy is sweet and mildly intoxicating, later fermenting into a sour fizzy drink much like champagne. My first taste of champagne (and a very fine one at that) evoked just that response from me—"but this is just like *kallu*!"

While coconut milk and ground coconut-based dishes may be easy to take to, cooking with coconut oil is another matter. The unique flavor of Kerala cuisine owes much to the smoky, nutty

29

flavor of coconut oil, but its flavor and scent are uncharted territory for the uninitiated who generally associate it with herbal hair oil. To begin with, try your standard fare with a hint of coconut oil; once you are convinced the difference is perceptible, you may be converted.

Coconuts are available in the market in many forms—as desiccated coconut, coconut cream, coconut milk powder, or concentrated coconut milk. However, nothing compares with the sweet crunch of a fresh coconut.

Cracking a coconut is an ordinary enough task in a Kerala kitchen, where a handheld coconut is split deftly into neat halves. But for the inexperienced, precise instructions are necessary: To crack a coconut, first remove the outer husk, pierce the eyes of the nut, and drain the juice. Then, using a heavy cleaver, strike it around the center, and crack the nut. Pry open the two halves and scrape the flesh off with a coconut scraper.

Visiting my newlywed niece Deepti and her husband, Appu, in Herndon, Virginia, I discovered it was coconut-cracking day, an act which left their apartment in shambles. Connoisseurs of authentic Kerala cooking, they had scoured the local markets and returned with their spoils, amazed at the impressive array of authentic ingredients they'd found: fine powdered rice for *puttu* and *appam*, fresh tapioca, silvery *karimeen* from the backwaters of Kottayam, *kodampuli* for fish curries, and rows of husked coconuts. With that problem solved, they then had to learn how to crack and open the coconuts. Back at home in India there were live-in helpers to teach them, but here in America, they relied on the Internet: "To crack a coconut …"

A year later, armed with a large cleaver and inspired Internet expertise, coconut cracking was still something of an ordeal for them. Later, when all was calm and we had swept the coconut shell shrapnel away, Deepti giggled as she showed me two smooth halves of coconut shells with the eyes gouged out. She had smuggled them over from India shrouded in the folds of a silky scarf when she had come to the United States a year earlier. These shells are used to steam *puttu* over the spout of a pressure cooker, working like a charm each time.

Extracting fresh coconut milk is, thankfully, a much easier task. Put the grated flesh of half a coconut in a blender with 1 cup of warm water. Soak for a few minutes and then turn the blender on. Blend until the coconut is well-puréed. Strain the mixture, pressing down on the coconut to extract all its milk. This is the 'first milk,' thick and creamy, and usually added to a curry in the last stages of cooking. 'Second milk' is extracted with two cups of warm water and the same coconut pulp as was used for the first extraction. Strain out the coconut and blend again for 'third milk,' if needed. Second and third milk are used in the early stages of curry making in place of water, so the fish, meat, or vegetable can fully absorb its flavor. The leftover milked coconut can be thrown away—but wait, it has its uses, too. The waste can be used as mulch for your plants. Truly, coconut is the fruit of the tree of life!

Recent newspaper stories on falling coconuts have given rise to much debate and are the topic of a report that won the Ig Nobel Prize, given annually at Harvard by the Editors of the Annals of Improbable Research. The debate still continues, but a travel insurance firm in England guarantees full coverage for travelers who get hit by falling coconuts. Though the actual number of deaths attributed to killer coconuts may be exaggerated, statistics reveal that a falling coconut weighing about 4 pounds, dropping 27 yards at a velocity of 50 miles per hour and with a force of about 1 ton on impact could indeed kill or render one comatose!

My own maternal grandmother Mamikutty's cousin was killed by a falling coconut while taking a nap under a coconut tree in his own grove—or so my mother once said.

Preparing Idiappam *(Stringhoppers, page 35)*

RICE AND RICE PREPARATIONS

The verdant paddy fields across Kerala bear witness to the importance of rice in the Malayali diet; it is the state's staple food. The Malayali way of saying "eat" is expressed *choru unnu*, similar to the Chinese *chi fan*—both literally meaning "eat rice."

From the long-grain basmati favored in the north to the short-grain *ponni* of the south, a wide variety of rice is grown in India. In Kerala, parboiled unpolished *matta* rice with its nutritious husk is preferred over the polished white rice popular elsewhere in India. *Matta* rice is boiled, dried, and then husked, retaining much of the bran, which gives this flavorsome rice its characteristic reddish hue. Parboiled rice is simmered over wood fires in smoky kitchen hearths all over the state, imbibing a distinctive, smoky flavor and aroma along the way.

Polished and unpolished rice is also ground to a paste, or alternately, powdered and roasted, to make a range of dishes. For example, ground rice paste is mixed with sour toddy (fermented coconut sap) and coconut to create soft, lacy *paalappams*, spongy *vattayappams*, and *kallappams* (fermented rice cakes). Roasted rice flour is steamed in large, hollow bamboo stems for *puttu* and mixed into doughs to prepare an assortment of sweet and savory snacks. Rice and all rice-based preparations are gluten-free and suitable for a gluten-free diet.

To make rice flours, rice is traditionally hand-pounded with *olakkas* (wooden paddles) and dry roasted in large *uralis* over wood fires—a laborious process that was once a part of life in a Syrian Christian home. However, with the advent of modern conveniences and the shortage of domestic help customary to that earlier way of life, many have abandoned smoky hearths for gas stoves and opt instead for pre-packaged, machine-ground rice flours to prepare *appams* and *puttu*.

Parboiled Rice
Puzhakkal Ari

The large, round reddish-brown grains of parboiled rice retain the nutritious bran which is stripped from polished white rice. Since it takes considerably longer to cook than polished rice, it should be pre-soaked for an hour or even longer. Once cooked the rice is soft and moist with a faintly nutty flavor. Though best cooked over a traditional wood fire where it acquires a smoky taste, parboiled rice can also be cooked on a stovetop.

Serves 2

1 cup parboiled rice*
6 cups water
½ teaspoon salt (*optional*)

Wash the rice and pre-soak in 2 cups of water for about an hour before cooking.

Bring the remaining water to a boil in a deep pot. Add the soaked rice grains along with the water and salt, if desired. Lower the heat to medium once the water is boiling again and cover with a lid. Cook for 15 minutes or until the rice is soft.

Remove from the heat and keep covered for about 15 minutes to allow the rice to swell. Drain any excess water.

*NOTE: Parboiled rice is also called 'converted rice.' The rice with the hull is soaked, partially cooked, then cooled and dried. This process allows the nutrients from the husk, bran and germ to permeate the grains of rice.

Stringhoppers
Idiappam

These steamed cakes made of fine strands of rice flour dough probably have their origins in the Far East and have been adapted to suit local tastes. In Kerala, an idiappam achu *(an idiappam maker) is used, but the dough can also be pressed with a fine ricer or vermicelli maker. Any type of steamer can be used to cook the* idiappam. *Serve with sweetened coconut milk or stew.*

Bring the water, oil, and salt to a boil in a deep pot. Once the water is boiling, lower the heat, slowly add the rice flour, and mix well. Remove from the heat and let the dough sit until it is cool enough to handle. On a smooth surface, knead the cooled dough well until it is soft, smooth, and free of lumps.

Bring water to a boil in the bottom pot of a steamer. Line a plate that fits into the steamer top with the banana leaves.

Put about 1 cup of dough in an *idiappam achu* or ricer or vermicelli maker and press the thin strands onto the banana leaves with a circular motion to form a small mound (see photo on page 32). Make three or four more mounds of dough in the same manner, spacing them on the banana leaves.

Sprinkle each mound of dough with 1 tablespoon of coconut. Place the plate in a steamer and steam for 5 minutes.

While the first batch is steaming, prepare the next batch on fresh banana leaves, until all the dough has been used.

Keep each batch of *idiappam* warm in an insulated serving dish as the next is being steamed.

Serves 4

2 cups water or thin coconut milk
1 tablespoon oil
½ teaspoon salt
3 cups fine unroasted rice flour
6 banana leaves, cleaned and lightly oiled
¼ cup grated fresh coconut

Rice Gruel
Kanji

A nutritious comfort food ideal for invalids and the elderly, kanji *is best made with broken parboiled rice cooked to a soft mush.* Kanji *is traditionally eaten in* kopas *(ceramic bowls) and is scooped up with little palm-leaf spoons. Farmworkers often eat this nourishing gruel with chutney or pickle as a mid-morning meal. As* kanji *is associated with humility and austerity, it is served during the Christian Holy Week.* Serve hot with sautéed mung beans, pappadams, *and chutney.*

Wash the rice, place in a medium saucepan, add the water, and pre-soak for an hour. Bring the rice and water to a slow boil. Reduce heat and simmer for 20 minutes or until the rice is soft; add extra water for a thinner gruel and salt, if desired.

Serves 2

1 cup coarsely broken parboiled rice
5 cups water
½ teaspoon salt (*optional*)

Rice Flatbread
Pathiri

Pathiri *is a soft, light bread borrowed from the Muslims of the Malabar region. It is served along with a coconut milk dipping sauce, which moistens and flavors the bread.* Serve with spicy chicken or mutton curry.

In a medium pot, bring the water with the salt and sugar to a boil. Add the rice flour, stirring well, and remove from the heat.

When cool enough to handle, knead the dough on a flat surface into a soft dough. Shape the dough into soft lime-size balls and roll these out into thin disks. Roast the flatbreads on a griddle for 1 minute on each side or until light brown spots appear. Fold into quarters and keep warm until serving. Serve with thick coconut milk for dipping.

Makes 12 to 15

2 cups water
½ teaspoon salt
½ teaspoon sugar
2 cups fine roasted rice flour
1 cup thick coconut milk for dipping sauce

Steamed Rice Cake
Puttu

Out of curiosity I asked a hundred Syrian Christians what their favorite food was, and it was no surprise that more than eighty of them said—"puttu!"

Puttu is prepared with roasted, coarsely ground rice flour and fresh, grated coconut. The rice flour is made with short-grained polished rice, which produces coarse white flour, or with parboiled rice, which produces a reddish-brown flour. Prepared rice flour—often labeled as puttu *flour—is available in both forms at Kerala grocery stores or on the Internet.*

Puttu is traditionally steamed in a puttu kuti, *but it can also be steamed in teacups or even empty coconut shells, in any type of steamer.*

The key to perfect puttu *is the rice flour mixture, which must be just moist enough to hold together. As with pastas and breads, the water needed for the dough varies, so you may have to add more if the mixture is too dry. Every housewife has a foolproof recipe for preparing perfect* puttu. *My sister Latha sieves the rice mix to get a soft, lump-free dough. A friend mixes the grated coconut with the flour, which, she says, produces a moister* puttu. *Do try both methods. In some parts of Kerala, the rice flour mixture is layered with curried meat or shrimp in an interesting variation.* Serve with bananas and paani, or with chickpea curry or stew.

Serves 4

1 cup water plus extra if needed
¼ teaspoon salt
3 cups roasted rice flour
½ cup grated fresh coconut

In a large bowl, combine the water, salt, and rice flour. Mix lightly until it has a crumbly consistency, sprinkling with extra water if needed. To test if the mixture has enough moisture, press a handful tight in a fist. The mixture should hold its shape. If it is too dry, sprinkle with more water and mix until it resembles coarse bread crumbs. Sieve the mixture to remove any lumps, cover and let sit for 1 hour.

Heat water in the bottom half of a steamer. In the upper cylinder of the *puttu* steamer (see Note below), put a tablespoon of coconut, then ½ cup of rice flour mixture. Continue making layers alternating the two until the container is almost filled, finishing with a layer of coconut.

Place over the steamer and steam for 3 to 5 minutes. Gently slide each batch of cooked *puttu* out of the cylinder, and then prepare the next batch. Keep each batch of *puttu* warm in an insulated serving dish while the next is being steamed.

NOTE: If using teacups or coconut shells, lightly grease them before using. Put 1 teaspoon of coconut into the cup or shell, then a ¼ cup of rice flour mixture; repeat with another teaspoon of coconut and a ¼ cup of rice flour mixture. Finally top this with 1 teaspoon of coconut. Fill the other containers in the same manner and then steam for 3 to 5 minutes.

Steamed Riceball Cakes
Mani Puttu

In this variation of the traditional puttu, *the rice flour mix is rolled into tiny pea-size balls, then steamed in the usual way. Serve with any curry or with sweetened coconut milk. These cakes can also be added to a* payasam, *such as Steamed Rice Paste Porridge (page 209), or to a Chicken Stew (page 127).*

In a large saucepan, bring the water with the salt and oil to a boil. Add the rice flour and stir until it becomes a soft dough. Remove from the heat and let it sit until cool enough to handle. On a flat surface, knead the cooled dough well, and shape it into pea-size balls.

Heat water in the bottom half of a steamer. In the upper cylinder of the *puttu* steamer (see Note), put 1 tablespoon of coconut, then ½ cup of the rice flour balls. Continue making layers, alternating the two until the cylinder is almost filled, finishing with a layer of coconut. Steam for 5 minutes or until cooked through.

Repeat process until all the dough balls are used. Keep each batch of *mani puttu* warm in an insulated serving dish, while the next is being steamed.

NOTE: Teacups or coconut shells can be used in place of the *puttu* cylinder, adjusting quantities used in each layer.

Serves 4

2 cups water
¼ teaspoon salt
1 tablespoon oil or butter
2 cups fine roasted rice flour
1 cup grated fresh coconut

Lace-Rimmed Pancakes

Paalappam

Everyone has a favorite recipe for this popular rice cake with its delicate, lacy rim. Ideally raised with coconut toddy, this recipe uses active dry yeast instead. In warm weather, the batter will rise in one hour, becoming light and frothy.

Paalappam *is traditionally made in an* appam chatti *over a wood fire hearth. The round bottom of the vessel helps create the "lace" and the heavy lid, which is heated, supplies the* appam *with dry heat from above. A wok or a skillet with a lid is an adequate substitute.*

Though paalappams *are really a breakfast food, they are ideal for a light lunch or dinner. Serve with sweetened coconut milk or stew.*

PREPARE THE BATTER:

In a food processor, grind the short-grain rice with 2 cups of water until smooth. Add the cooked rice and process for a few more minutes until the batter is thick and smooth.

Pour the batter into a large bowl that holds about three times its volume. Mix in the coconut milk, salt, and sugar. Combine the yeast and warm milk, and stir into the rice batter. Cover and set aside for an hour or longer, until the batter has risen and is lightly fermented. Then thin the batter with 2 cups of water or more to get a runny consistency.

PREPARE THE PAALAPPAMS:

Lightly grease an *appam chatti* or wok and heat over a high flame. Lower the heat to medium and pour a ½ cup of batter into the pan, slowly swirling it around so the batter coats the pan and then settles into the center.

Cover and cook until the *appam* is firm and the surrounding "lace" is golden brown. Gently slide the *appam* out from the pan onto a plate and repeat the process until you have finished all of the batter.

Keep each *appam* warm in an insulated serving dish while the next is being prepared.

Serves 4

3 cups short-grain rice, soaked in water for 2 hours and then drained
2 cups water, plus about 2 cups for thinning
½ cup cooked rice
2 cups thick coconut milk
½ teaspoon salt
3 tablespoons sugar
1 teaspoon active dry yeast
¼ cup warm milk

NOTE: Some leftover batter can be stored in your refrigerator to ferment your next batch of *appams*. To use, let the 'sourdough' sit at room temperature for 3 to 4 hours before adding it to the new batter. You can then omit the yeast, but follow the rest of the recipe.

Lace-Rimmed Pancakes Made with Rice Flour

Paalappam made with Ari Podi

This paalappam *recipe uses unroasted rice flour instead of ground rice and is easier to prepare.*

Serves 4

PREPARE THE BATTER:

Mix the rice flour, yeast, sugar, and salt in a deep bowl. Add 2 cups of the warm water and mix well.

Put the cooked rice and remaining 1 cup of warm water in a blender or food processor and grind to a paste. Add to the rice-flour batter.

Add the coconut milk and mix well. Cover and set aside in a warm place for an hour or longer, until the batter has risen and is lightly fermented. Then add 1 cup of water or more to get a runny consistency.

PREPARE THE PAALAPPAMS:

Lightly grease an *appam chatti* or wok and heat over a high flame. Then lower to medium heat and pour a ½ cup of batter into the pan. Swirl the batter around, so the batter coats the pan and then settles into the center.

Cover and cook until the *appam* is firm and the surrounding "lace" is golden brown. Gently slide out the *appam* from the pan onto a plate and repeat the process until you have finished all the batter.

Keep the *appams* warm in an insulated serving dish while the others are being prepared.

3 cups fine unroasted rice flour
1 teaspoon active dry yeast
¼ cup sugar
¼ teaspoon salt
3 cups warm water, plus 1 cup for thinning
¼ cup cooked rice
1 cup thick coconut milk

Steamed Rice Batter Cake
Vattayappams

Vattayappams *are similar in taste to* paalappams, *but have a spongier consistency. They can be made ahead and stored in the refrigerator for up to a week. Serve hot or cold with curries and stews, or alternately, with* paani *as a sweet dish or snack.*

In a medium saucepan, mix ½ cup warm water and the semolina and simmer to make a gruel. Set aside.

In a blender or food processor, grind the grated coconut with 1 cup of the warm water to make a smooth paste.

Mix the rice flour, yeast, sugar, and salt in a deep bowl. Add the remaining 1½ cups of warm water, the coconut paste, and the gruel and mix well. Cover and set aside to rise in a warm place for an hour or longer. When it is lightly fermented, the batter should be frothy and thick, like cake batter.

Grease three shallow heatproof pans about 6 inches in diameter and divide the batter among them. Place in a steamer and steam the batter for about 20 minutes or until firm. Remove and cut into wedges.

Serves 4

3 cups warm water
½ cup semolina (cream of wheat)
1 cup grated fresh coconut
3 cups fine unroasted rice flour
1 teaspoon active dry yeast
3 tablespoons sugar
½ teaspoon salt

VARIATION: Add extra sugar or honey, raisins and fried cashews to the batter for a light gluten-free dessert cake.

Toddy Pancakes

Kallappams

As the name implies, these appams *get their name from* kallu, *the toddy that is traditionally used to prepare the batter. Yeast is substituted here, with good results.* Kallappams *are cooked on a griddle like thick pancakes. Serve these pancakes hot or cold with curries and stews. Or they can be served with traditional pancake accompaniments like maple syrup, honey, or jams.*

Grind the soaked rice with the 2 cups of water in a blender or food processor until it becomes a smooth batter. Add the coconut and cooked rice, and process for 2 more minutes.

Pour the batter into a deep bowl and add the sugar, salt, and yeast mixture. Set aside to rise in a warm place for an hour or longer. When ready, the mixture should be like a frothy cake batter.

Pour ¾ cup of batter on a hot, lightly greased griddle, and cook the thick pancakes over medium heat for 1 minute on each side. Repeat until all the batter has been used, keeping the cooked pancakes warm.

Makes 16

3 cups short-grain rice, soaked in water for 2 hours and then drained
2 cups water
1 cup grated fresh coconut
¼ cup cooked rice
3 tablespoons sugar
¼ teaspoon salt
1 teaspoon active dry yeast, soaked in ¼ cup warm water

Passover Bread
Pesha Appam / INRI Appam

This steamed rice bread is perhaps one of the few foods that link the Syrian Christian community to the Levant, and to the early Syrians and Jews. The preparation of this unleavened bread is a sacred ceremony and ritual has to be followed. Once the batter is made the palm leaves from Palm Sunday are folded in a cross that is placed on the batter before steaming.

Passover Bread is prepared on Maundy Thursday (Pesaha Vyazham), the fifth day of Holy Week. In a re-enactment of the Last Supper, when Jesus broke bread with the twelve apostles, a family elder will lead the appam murikkal *with a short prayer and divides the unleavened rice bread among family members, which is then dipped into a sweetened co-conut milk sauce (*pesaha paal*).*

Soak the black gram in water for 2 hours. Drain and grind to a fine paste, using just enough water in the process to form a batter. Put the batter in a mixing bowl along with the rice flour.

Grind the coconut, shallots, garlic, and cumin seeds just enough to make a coarse paste and combine with the batter. Add the salt. The batter should be similar to a pancake batter—if it is too thick add a few tablespoons of coconut milk to thin it. Set aside to rest for an hour.

Pour the batter into a greased pan. Cut a section of palm leaf and form a cross in the center of the batter. Steam for 20 minutes and set aside to cool. Serve with the *pesaha paal.*

PREPARE THE PESAHA PAAL:
Heat the coconut milk and jaggery till well blended. Mix the rice flour with enough water to make a smooth paste. Add this to the coconut milk and stir continously till it has thickened to a smooth syrup. Take off the heat and immediately stir in the spices while it is still warm.

Makes 1 loaf

¼ cup black gram (urad beans), shelled
1½ cups rice flour
1 cup grated coconut
4 shallots
1 clove garlic
¼ teaspoon cumin seeds
¼ teaspoon salt

PESAHA PAAL (COCONUT SYRUP)
3 cups thick coconut milk
1½ cups finely grated jaggery
¼ cup rice flour
¼ teaspoon dried ginger
⅓ teaspoon roasted cumin seeds
½ teaspoon cardamom powder

The Granary *Nellu Ara*

Most houses in the backwaters and in the towns nearby have large wooden granaries used to store rice for the year. Once the paddy is harvested, the rice is boiled, dried, and husked before being stored in the confines of these wooden rooms. The *nellu ara* may vary in size from a large, carved, box-like room with a stout wooden door as is found in houses situated in town, to multi-storied structures in larger homes located in the agricultural areas. The granaries are made of jack tree wood and elaborately carved and decorated, often with a large, intricately fashioned lock on the door. Legends of hidden treasures and pots of gold buried deep in the granaries of aristocratic homes fired our imagination when we were children.

In my maternal grandparents' house in the town of Allepey, a large *nellu ara* sat in the middle of a dark room near the kitchens, where the beautiful, carved walls of the granary were seen only by the women and servants rushing about their daily chores. As children, we ran around the *nellu ara* playing hide-and-seek, ducking behind corners that were perfect for surprise attacks. This particular *nellu ara* stood on thick wooden legs, and the most nimble could even slide under it to where no light could penetrate.

Earlier this year while working on my book, I visited my maternal grandmother's ancestral home—the Velliyara Parayil *tharavad* in Thycattassery. The grand old home of this ancient family, whose ancestors were once titled chevaliers and a marquis, now stood forlorn and empty, its vast hallways echoing my footsteps. The imposing house still held traces of its old grandeur but was showing signs of neglect. As I walked through the empty rooms, various images flitted through my mind. Here my grandmother as a motherless toddler took her first steps. Here also was the courtyard where she played hopscotch. Was this the room where she had worn her first *chatta* and *mundu* and pleated her first fantail? There was the bathing room with a hearth for a wood fire where a cauldron of water must have simmered while she and her sisters were massaged with herbal oils. Now, cobwebs and a thick layer of dust covered every surface.

In the heart of this three-hundred-year-old house stood the double-storied granary. I was pleased to find the carved walls of the old *nellu ara* still dark and solid, the ornate brass lock gleaming on the heavy door that swung open on wooden hinges. This was one of the granaries that allegedly held a treasure in its dark recesses, hidden behind a secret trapdoor. But the *ara* was empty; its walls told me no tales, and the trapdoor opened to a dark, musty cavern.

Mutton Biryani
Atterachi Biryani

Biryani *is the ultimate food of feasts all over India. This sumptuous dish, originating in the Middle East, appears in many variations. A meal in one, it contains meat cooked into a rich* korma *and layered with rice and whole spices.* Biryanis *are traditionally cooked over a wood fire. The vessel is sealed tight around the lid with a thick paste of dough and live coals are placed on the lid. But an oven works almost as well, with a cup of water poured over the lid of the vessel to keep the* biryani *moist.*

A biryani *can never be hastily prepared. To achieve a perfect* biryani, *each ingredient must be carefully measured and every stage of cooking planned. Although the shorter-grain* ponni *rice is preferred in Southern India, long-grain rice is best for a biryani. In this Malayali version, rich coconut milk and meat stock adds great flavor to the rice.*

Serve with an onion and yogurt salad, date chutney, and pappadams.

PREPARE THE RICE:

Heat the ghee in a deep pot, add the rice and cinnamon and sauté for a few minutes, until the rice is well-coated with the ghee. Add the water and salt and cook uncovered over low heat until the water has been absorbed—the rice will only be half-cooked. Spread out on a tray.

PREPARE THE KORMA:

Heat the oil in a large wok, add the onions, and fry for 3 to 5 minutes, until they turn dark brown. Add the ginger and garlic pastes and fry for 1 minute, stirring continuously. Add one at a time the green chillis, cashew butter, and yogurt, stirring and frying for 1 minute after each addition.

When the oil rises to the top, add the ground coriander, turmeric, chilli powder, cardamom and cloves. Fry

continued on next page

Serves 8

RICE:
¼ cup ghee
6 cups uncooked long-grain rice
3 (2-inch) cinnamon sticks
8 cups water
1 teaspoon salt

KORMA:
½ cup oil
4 onions, thinly sliced
1 tablespoon ginger paste
3 tablespoons garlic paste
4 green chillis, seeded and chopped
¼ cup cashew butter
1 cup plain yogurt
¼ cup ground coriander
1 teaspoon ground turmeric
1 teaspoon chilli powder
6 cardamom pods, crushed
6 whole cloves
2 pounds mutton (goat meat) or lamb, cubed*
1 cup chopped fresh coriander (cilantro)
¼ cup chopped fresh mint
1 tablespoon salt
6 cups water
2 tablespoons lime juice

continued on next page

this mixture for a few minutes, stirring continuously to prevent the spices from sticking to the wok.

Add the mutton cubes and mix until the meat is coated with the spice mixture. Add the fresh coriander, mint, salt, and water. Simmer for 20 minutes or until the meat is tender, adding more water if necessary. The gravy should be reduced until there is about 1 cup left. Then stir the lime juice into the meat.

ASSEMBLE THE BIRYANI:

Preheat the oven to 325 degrees F.

Divide the half-cooked rice into three portions. Spread one portion to cover the bottom of a 10-inch square deep ovenproof dish. Cover the rice with half of the cooked mutton. Spread another layer of rice on top, and then cover with the rest of the mutton. Finally, top the meat with the last portion of rice.

Poke holes in the mixture with a skewer. Combine the coconut milk and meat stock, and pour evenly over the rice. Drizzle the ghee over and into the rice. Cover the dish with a heavy concave lid or place the lid on upside down so it can hold water; pour 1 cup of water over the lid. Place in the oven and bake for 30 minutes and then let it rest for 10 minutes before serving.

PREPARE THE GARNISH:

Heat the ghee in a medium skillet and fry the onions until they are a golden brown. Remove the onions from the pan and fry the cashews, adding the raisins as the nuts brown. Remove from the heat as soon as the raisins swell up. Garnish the *biryani* with the fried onions, cashews, and raisins.

TO ASSEMBLE:
2 cups thick coconut milk
2 cups meat stock
¼ cup ghee

TO GARNISH:
3 tablespoons ghee
1 large onion, thinly sliced
12 cashews
¼ cup raisins

*NOTE: Though mutton and lamb are the preferred meats for a *biryani*, meats like chicken, beef and turkey are good substitutes.

Shrimp Biryani
Chemmeen Biryani

This is a light seafood biryani, *in which rice is simmered along with the sautéed shrimp—a different method from the layered biryani which uses half-cooked rice. This recipe can be used to prepare meat and chicken* biryanis, *and is also tasty when made with fillets of fish. Serve with a raw onion and tomato salad.*

Heat the oil in a large skillet. Add the shallots and sauté until they turn a light brown. One at a time add the ginger paste, garlic paste, green chillis, and chopped tomatoes, stirring and frying for 1 minute after each ingredient is added. Add the turmeric, chilli powder, and crushed peppercorns; sauté until the oil rises to the top.

Add the shrimp and salt, and cook until the shrimp are coated with the spices. Add the coconut milk, fresh coriander, and lime juice, and cook over a low flame for 5 minutes. Remove from the heat and set aside.

Heat the ghee in a deep, heavy pot and add the rice, cardamom pods, and cloves. Stir until the grains of rice are coated with the ghee, and then stir the shrimp mixture into the fried rice. Pour the water into the pot, cover with a lid, and simmer over low heat for 25 to 30 minutes or until the rice is done.

PREPARE THE GARNISH: Heat the ghee in a medium skillet and fry the onion until golden brown. Remove the onion from the pan and fry the cashews until they are lightly browned.

Let the biryani sit for 10 minutes before serving. Garnish with the fried onions and cashew nuts.

Serves 8

¼ cup oil
20 shallots, sliced
1 tablespoon ginger paste
3 tablespoons garlic paste
6 whole green chillis
3 tomatoes, chopped
1 teaspoon ground turmeric
1 teaspoon chilli powder
½ teaspoon crushed black peppercorns
2 pounds large shrimp, shelled and deveined
1 tablespoon salt
1 cup thick coconut milk
½ cup chopped fresh coriander (cilantro)
2 tablespoons lime juice
¼ cup ghee
6 cups long-grain rice
6 cardamom pods, crushed
6 whole cloves
12 cups water

GARNISH:
3 tablespoons ghee
1 large onion, thinly sliced
12 cashews

Traditional Paddy Cultivation

In Kerala, different varieties of rice are cultivated on wet and dry level land. Some yield three crops a year, whereas some produce only one. The highest yields range from twenty to seventy-fold. Methods of cultivation are a combination of the traditional, whereby the farmer still relies on the ancient methods used by his ancestors, and the modern, with new implements and motorized equipment. *Kerala Kalpam* (an ancient Sanskrit manuscript on agriculture) is taught in village schools even today, and in it traditional methods of cultivation are advocated in verse.

The first sowing of the paddy for each year, which commences with ceremonial prayers to the gods, takes place during the festival of Vishu, the Malayali New Year's Day, just before the monsoons. The day Vishu falls on is said to determine the harvest—if, for instance, it falls on a Monday, the fields should receive three measures of rain and the harvest should be rich and abundant.

Most fields in the often rain-drenched state of Kerala are supplemented by alluvial deposits washed down from the mountains each monsoon and need little manure. The soil is turned with large, iron-tipped plows led by bulls or buffalo that plow in the cow manure, ashes, and leaves left there previously to decompose. It is important, the *Kerala Kalpam* advises, to entice the bulls with song and not to prod them with sticks and harsh words. Sowing is done by hand and this—the manuscript counsels—should be done with a song in the heart or on the lips of the farmers. The seedlings, raised in other fields or in seed beds, are transplanted to these compost-rich fields when they reach maturity. At each stage, prayers are offered to the gods: for the seeds to yield generously, for timely showers, and finally, for good sunshine and a plentiful harvest.

Interestingly, this ancient manuscript also advises that only men of a calm and orderly disposition should take up agriculture, stating that a man contrary to this type should not do so.

Lentils, beans, and grains at a Kerala market

VEGETABLES, BEANS, AND LENTILS

Syrian Christian cuisine has become synonymous with appams, fish curries, and meat stews, but its vegetarian dishes are just as distinctive. Malayali cuisine boasts an extensive range of vegetarian preparations, each cooked in different combinations of ginger, garlic, yogurt, and coconut. Little or no water is used and the vegetables cook in their own juices. Shallots, with their subtle flavor, the aromatic curry leaf, and the fiery, miniature kandhari chillis or the tamer green chillis are used as seasoning.

A variety of exotic vegetables and greens endemic to this region are often combined with regular fare such as carrots, potatoes, and green beans. Slender string beans, banana flowers, colocassi (taro), drumstick greens, papaya, jackfruit seeds, yams, tapioca, breadfruit, pumpkin, bitter gourd, snake gourd, and a host of other gourds are some of these. Other unusual favorites include the koorka (*coleus tuber*), a smallish bulb with a hairy skin that is thrashed in a sack to strip the peel, and the long drumstick beans (*moringa oleifera*), which really do resemble drumsticks.

Lentils and beans are cooked on their own or with vegetables and coconut. Vegetable dishes are eaten with rice and accompaniments like buttermilk, *pappadams*, and chutney for vegetarian meals or as side dishes along with meat and fish dishes. Many of these dishes—*thoran, avial, kaalen, thiyal, olan, pachadi, erisseri,* and *parippu*—feature in a *sadya*, a vegetarian feast of rice, vegetable and lentil dishes traditionally served on a banana leaf during festive occasions like *Onam* (the harvest festival).

All the recipes in this chapter are vegan (dairy yogurt can be substituted with cashew yogurt or any other vegan yogurt).

Spinach with Crushed Coconut
Cheera Thoran

A thoran, prepared with a coarse crush of coconut, chillis, and ginger, can be made with any vegetable—cabbage, green beans, snake gourd, banana flowers, or even unripe papaya. I have also made thorans *with chopped green onions, mushrooms, and green tomatoes—all equally delicious. The vegetable(s) should be finely shredded or chopped and lightly mixed with the coconut mixture. It is then cooked in a covered pot with little or no water so the vegetable steams in its own juices. Serve as a side dish with rice, thiyal, and accompaniments.*

In a medium bowl, mix the spinach with the salt and coconut paste, and set aside.

Heat the oil in a medium skillet and add the mustard seeds. When the seeds burst, add the shallots, curry leaves, and red chillis and sauté lightly.

Add the spinach mixture to the skillet and sprinkle with a little water. Cover and cook until the water has evaporated.

Serves 2

4 cups chopped spinach
½ teaspoon salt
1 teaspoon oil
½ teaspoon mustard seeds
6 shallots, sliced
6 curry leaves
2 red chillis, torn in half

COCONUT PASTE

Grind to a coarse paste:
½ cup grated fresh coconut
½ teaspoon ground turmeric
1 green chilli, chopped
1 teaspoon chopped fresh ginger
2 cloves garlic
½ teaspoon cumin seeds

Potato Sauté

Kezhangu Varathathu

This is a Keralite version of the potato dish that is a classic in every regional cuisine of India. Coconut oil gives this dish a uniquely Malayali flavor, but any other oil can be used instead. Serve with rice, parippu, and accompaniments, as a side dish.

In a large pot, boil the potatoes in about 6 cups of water with the salt, turmeric, and ground chillis for 5 minutes. When the potatoes are parboiled, remove from the heat, drain and set aside to cool.

Heat the oil in a medium skillet and sauté the onion for 1 minute or until soft and translucent. Add the garlic and curry leaves and continue frying over low heat for 1 minute.

Add the crushed peppercorns and potatoes and stir-fry until the potatoes are crisp and golden.

Serves 2

3 large potatoes, cut into 1-inch cubes
1 teaspoon salt
½ teaspoon ground turmeric
3 red chillis, coarsely ground
¼ cup coconut oil
1 large onion, sliced
3 cloves garlic, sliced
6 curry leaves
1 teaspoon crushed black peppercorns

Mixed Vegetable Curry
Avial

Avial *literally means a "mix-up." This is a mixed vegetable dish with a thick coconut and yogurt gravy and cubes of raw mango for added piquancy. It is important not to stir the dish with a spoon, as it may break up the vegetables. Instead, shake and swirl the pot to mix. Serve as a main dish with rice, pickles, and* pappadams.

Put the 3 cups of vegetables in a shallow pan. Add the coconut paste, water, and salt. Cover and cook over medium heat for 10 minutes, adding the drumstick bean and mango halfway through the cooking.

When the vegetables are cooked, set aside to cool until lukewarm. Add the yogurt and carefully toss the vegetables to coat.

Heat the oil in a small skillet and add the mustard seeds. As they burst, add the curry leaves and fry until they are crisp. Pour the oil with seasonings into the cooked *avial*. Serve at room temperature.

NOTE: Do not reheat this dish.

Serves 4

3 cups diced, mixed vegetables—any combination of carrots, potatoes, bananas, beans, eggplants, and yams
4 cups water
1 tablespoon salt
1 drumstick bean, cut into 2-inch pieces
¼ cup diced green mango
1 cup thick (Greek) plain yogurt, lightly beaten
1 tablespoon coconut oil
1 teaspoon mustard seeds
6 curry leaves

COCONUT PASTE

Grind to a fine paste:
½ cup grated fresh coconut
2 green chillis
1 teaspoon chopped fresh ginger
1 teaspoon ground cumin
½ teaspoon ground turmeric
1 teaspoon mustard seeds

Jackfruit Seed, Cooked and Fried

Chakka Kuru Olathiathu

The seeds of the ripe jackfruit are savored by Malayalis for their crisp, nutty flavor and hint of sweetness. The tough outer shell can easily be peeled, which leaves a thinner skin that need not be removed. Jackfruit seeds can also be roasted over hot coals and seasoned with salt and chilli powder. The seed resembles a miniature egg and is used in colloquial language to describe someone who is airheaded or scatterbrained. Serve as a side dish or as a snack.

In a medium pot, cook the sliced jackfruit seeds in the 3 cups of water with the ground chillis, turmeric, peppercorns, and salt for 5 to 8 minutes. When the water has evaporated, and the seeds are cooked, remove from the heat and set aside.

Heat the oil in a medium skillet and fry the shallots, adding the garlic and curry leaves as the shallots brown.

Add the cooked jackfruit seeds and stir-fry over low heat for 2 to 3 minutes, until the seeds are lightly browned.

Serves 3 to 4

2 cups sliced jackfruit seeds
3 cups water
3 red chillis, coarsely ground
½ teaspoon ground turmeric
½ teaspoon crushed black peppercorns
½ teaspoon salt
2 teaspoons coconut oil
½ cup sliced shallots
3 cloves garlic, crushed
6 curry leaves

Unripe Bananas, Cooked and Fried

Vazhakka Olathiathu

Though the thick outer skin of the banana is usually removed, my mother often cooked it with the skin, which gives the dish a special crunch. Serve with rice, thoran, *and spiced buttermilk.*

Pare and discard the outer skin of the bananas. Cut the fruit into 1-inch rectangular pieces. Put them into a bowl of water to prevent discoloration, then rinse and drain before using.

Place the banana pieces in a pan with the 2 cups of water, turmeric, and salt, and cook for 5 to 6 minutes over low heat, until the water has evaporated.

Heat the oil in a medium skillet and add the mustard seeds. When they burst, add the shallots. Sauté for 2 to 3 minutes until brown, then add the garlic, curry leaves, ground chillis, and crushed peppercorns.

Add the cooked banana, mix, and cook for 1 minute, stirring continuously.

Serves 2

4 unripe green bananas
2 cups water, plus extra for soaking the bananas
¼ teaspoon ground turmeric
½ teaspoon salt
2 tablespoons oil
½ teaspoon mustard seeds
4 shallots, sliced
4 cloves garlic, crushed
6 curry leaves
2 red chillis, coarsely ground
4 peppercorns, crushed

Mashed and Seasoned Tapioca
Kappa Purattiathu

Kappa *is daily fare in tea stalls and toddy shops all over Kerala, and a staple food of farm laborers. Though it can be eaten plain, there is nothing more satisfying than a plate of seasoned, mashed tapioca and fish curry—the soft mound of* kappa *perfectly complementing the sour, spicy fish. Malayalis who live in distant places get nostalgic about this sublime combination, one that brings back memories of smoky kitchens back home. Breadfruit can also be prepared using this recipe.* Serve as a side dish with fish curry or fried meat.

Put the tapioca in a deep pot with the salt and add enough water to cover. Cook for 30 minutes or until soft. Remove from the heat.

While the tapioca is still hot stir in the coconut paste and mash coarsely with a potato masher. Set aside.

Heat the oil in a small skillet and add the mustard seeds. When they burst, add the shallots and fry until lightly browned. Stir in the curry leaves and red chillis and remove from the heat. Pour this mixture with its oil into the mashed tapioca and mix well.

Serves 4

2 pounds fresh tapioca, peeled and cubed
1 tablespoon salt
2 tablespoons coconut oil
1 tablespoon mustard seeds
6 shallots, sliced
8 curry leaves
3 red chillis, halved

COCONUT PASTE

Grind to a coarse paste:
1 cup grated fresh coconut
1 tablespoon chopped fresh ginger
½ teaspoon ground turmeric
½ teaspoon cumin seeds
4 shallots
2 green chillis

NOTE: Leftover seasoned tapioca can be shaped into cutlets, stuffed with coconut chutney, and covered with crumbs and pan-fried.

Big Sister Dove and Little Sister Dove

Kuttathi prave, kurr, kurr
Nazhi payare, kurr, kurr
Little sister dove, kurr, kurr
A measure of beans, kurr, kurr

Once upon a time deep in the forests of Kerala, there lived two sister doves—Vallia kuttathi pravu and Kochu kuttathi pravu. Their parents had flown away in search of food and never returned. All alone now, Big Sister Dove would bring food to their little cave and Little Sister Dove would cook it. The sisters adjusted to life without their parents and were happy.

One day, Big Sister Dove brought home some string beans and asked her sister to cook them for their meal. Now everyone knows that *achinga payar* have to be sorted and cleaned before they can be used. The tough-skinned ones are shelled and only the tender beans can be cooked. This was exactly what Little Sister Dove did, leaving only a little clawful of the choicest, tender beans for her sister.

When Big Sister Dove came for their meal, she saw that only a few beans remained and became enraged, thinking that her little sister had eaten up most of them herself. Big Sister Dove grabbed her sister with her beak and hurled her into the fire, killing her instantly.

The next day, a wise old owl came and asked Big Sister Dove where her little sister was. Still feeling angry, she told the owl about how her little sister had selfishly eaten all the beans.

"But no," the owl said. "Little Sister Dove was only doing her duty by sorting the beans. And she had saved the most tender ones for you."

To this day, Big Sister Dove coos in anguish, remembering forever her thoughtless deed.

Kuttathi prave, kurr, kurr
Nazhi payare, kurr, kurr.

—An old Malayalam folktale, narrated by my mother

String Bean Sauté

Achinga Payar Olathiathu

This slender green string bean, a favorite with all Malayalis, is often called Kerala beans in vegetable markets out of the state. It is also the bean featured in the fable of the two doves, so don't be surprised if after cleaning and sorting, you end up with just half the beans you started with. Do not cut the beans with a knife; instead, break them with your hands so you will know if they are tender. If they are not, just use the tiny beans inside, discarding the shells. This recipe can also be used for green cluster beans. Serve with rice, ripe mango curry, and accompaniments.

Cook the string beans in a shallow pan with the water, ground chillis, turmeric, and salt. When the water has evaporated, set aside.

Heat the oil in a medium skillet and add the shallots, garlic, and curry leaves. Fry for 1 to 2 minutes, until lightly browned.

Add the cooked beans to the skillet and stir-fry for 2 minutes or until the beans are coated with the oil and shallot mixture.

Serves 2

2 cups string beans, broken into 1-inch-long pieces
1 cup water
2 red chillis, coarsely ground
½ teaspoon ground turmeric
½ teaspoon salt
1 tablespoon oil
6 shallots, sliced
3 cloves garlic, crushed
6 curry leaves

Fresh Cashew Sauté

Pacha Kashu Andi Olathiathu

In Kerala, fresh cashews just picked from cashew plantations are sold by women who bring the soft, unroasted nuts around to homes to be cooked immediately. If the skins are still on the nuts, peel them off with a sharp knife. Ask your local Indian grocery store for frozen unroasted cashews which are just as good. *Serve as a snack or as a side dish.*

Mix the cashews with the red chilli flakes, turmeric, peppercorns, and salt, and set aside.

Heat the oil in a skillet or wok. Add the shallots and fry for 1 minute until soft and translucent. Add the garlic and curry leaves, fry lightly, and add the spiced cashews. Stir-fry over medium heat for 3 to 4 minutes, until the cashews are browned and the spices well-cooked.

Serves 2

2 cups unroasted cashews
½ teaspoon dried red chilli flakes
¼ teaspoon ground turmeric
½ teaspoon crushed black peppercorns
½ teaspoon salt
1 tablespoon coconut oil
½ cup sliced shallots
½ teaspoon crushed garlic
6 curry leaves

VARIATIONS: I often combine strips of tender coconut with the fresh cashew in this recipe—a sublime combination. I also use this recipe to make Coconut Sauté using strips of tender but firm coconut.

Shallots with Tamarind and Roasted Coconut

Ulli Thiyal

This sour, spicy dish combines toasted coconut and tamarind with the sweetness of whole shallots. The coconut must be perfectly browned for a perfectly prepared thiyal. It is an ideal side dish for a vegetarian meal. Serve with rice, avial, *and accompaniments.*

Dry roast the coconut over medium heat in a heavy skillet, stirring continuously for 8 to 10 minutes, until it turns a dark brown color. Add the ginger and garlic and continue stirring. Stir in 8 of the red chillis, the peppercorns, and turmeric and remove from heat immediately. Set aside to cool. Once the mixture is cool, grind it together with a ½ cup water to make a fine paste.

Heat the oil in the same skillet and fry the shallots for 1 to 2 minutes, until they are soft and transparent.

Add the curry leaves and remaining 2 red chillis. Cook, stirring, for a few minutes, then add the coconut mixture. Continue frying, stirring continuously, until the oil rises to the top.

Add the tamarind paste, salt, and the remaining 1 cup of water and cook for 2 minutes or until the mixture thickens.

Serves 2

½ cup grated fresh coconut
½ teaspoon grated fresh ginger
1 teaspoon crushed garlic
10 red chillis, halved
6 black peppercorns
½ teaspoon ground turmeric
1½ cups water
2 teaspoons oil
2 cups peeled whole shallots
8 curry leaves
¼ cup tamarind paste
1 teaspoon salt

VARIATIONS: A *thiyal* can also be made with other ingredients like potatoes, unripe bananas, drumsticks, or bittergourds.

Wild Mushroom Sauté

Koon Olathiathu

Wild mushrooms, picked fresh from the fields and forests after the rains, are best used in this simple dish, but cultivated field and button mushrooms can be substituted. If using larger mushrooms, slice lengthwise before cooking. Serve on crisp toast for a light breakfast.

Heat the oil in a medium skillet, add the shallots and fry for 1 to 2 minutes, until light brown. Add the green chillis and curry leaves and fry for 1 minute.

Add the mushrooms, salt, and peppercorns, and cook until the juices evaporate. The mushrooms should be just cooked and coated with the spiced juices.

Serves 2

1 teaspoon coconut oil
½ cup sliced shallots
2 green chillis, cut in long thin slivers
6 curry leaves
2 cups whole wild mushrooms*
½ teaspoon salt
¼ teaspoon crushed black peppercorns

*NOTE: Don't just stick to one kind of mushroom for this recipe, use a variety of wild or cultivated mushrooms for a variety of flavors and textures.

Elephant Foot Yams with Ground Coconut

Chena Erisseri

Serve this dish as part of a vegetarian meal with rice and other vegetable dishes.

In a medium pot, cook the yams* in the 2 cups of water mixed with the salt for 8 to 10 minutes, until they are soft. Mash the yams with any remaining water with a potato masher.

Add the coconut paste to the yams and, if necessary, add water to get a runny consistency. Cook for 2 minutes, until the coconut mixture has blended in.

Heat the oil in a small skillet and add the mustard seeds. When they burst, add the shallots and sauté for 2 to 3 minutes or until browned. Add the red chillis, curry leaves, and grated coconut. Remove from heat and stir the seasoned oil with the spices into the cooked yams.

*NOTE: Yams can produce an itchy sensation in the mouth if not prepared before cooking. Soak the pieces of peeled yam in a mix of water and tamarind or buttermilk for an hour before cooking.

Serves 4

1 pound elephant foot yams, peeled and
  cut into 1-inch cubes*
2 cups water
1 tablespoon salt
2 teaspoons oil
1 teaspoon mustard seeds
6 shallots, sliced
2 red chillis, halved
8 curry leaves
1 tablespoon grated fresh coconut

COCONUT PASTE

Grind to a coarse paste:
½ cup grated fresh coconut
½ teaspoon ground turmeric
2 green chillis
1 teaspoon cumin seeds

Red Beans and Pumpkin in Coconut Milk

Olan

This is a mildly flavored curry that perfectly complements a spicier dish. If white pumpkin is unavailable at your local Indian grocery, try zucchini, which is close in flavor and texture. Serve as a side dish in a vegetarian meal, or with spicy meat dishes.

In a medium saucepan, cook the cowpeas in the thin coconut milk with the green chillis, cumin, and salt for 25 to 30 minutes, until they are soft.

Add the white pumpkin and continue cooking for 5 more minutes, adding water if needed. Stir in the thick coconut milk, remove from heat, and set aside.

Heat the oil in a small skillet and add the mustard seeds. When they burst, add the shallots and curry leaves and fry for 1 to 2 minutes, until light brown.

Stir the seasoned oil with the spices into the cowpea mixture. Reheat until warmed through but do not let it boil.

Serves 4

½ cup dried red cowpeas, soaked in water overnight
3 cups thin coconut milk
2 green chillis, slit
¼ teaspoon ground cumin
1 teaspoon salt
2 cups ½-inch cubes white pumpkin*
½ cup thick coconut milk
1 teaspoon oil
½ teaspoon mustard seeds
6 shallots, sliced
6 curry leaves

*NOTE: Though white pumpkin is traditionally used for this recipe, it can be substituted with red pumpkin which gives it a more robust flavor.

Sweet-and-Sour Ginger Curry

Inji Puli

This curry, almost a pickle, will keep for up to a week, and in fact tastes better after a few days. Serve with rice, thoran, and accompaniments.

Serves 4

Heat the oil in a small skillet and add the mustard seeds. When they burst, add the shallots and fry for 2 to 3 minutes or until light brown.

Lower the heat and add the fenugreek seeds, ginger, red chillis, and curry leaves. Fry for 2 minutes.

Add the chilli powder and turmeric and heat for 1 minute, stirring continuously so the spices are well-blended.

Add the tamarind paste, brown sugar, and salt and cook for 2 to 3 minutes, until the curry is thick.

¼ cup oil
1 teaspoon mustard seeds
6 shallots, thinly sliced
½ teaspoon fenugreek seeds
1 cup thin slices fresh ginger
3 red chillis, torn in half
6 curry leaves
1 tablespoon chilli powder
½ teaspoon ground turmeric
¼ cup tamarind paste
3 tablespoons jaggery or dark brown sugar
1 teaspoon salt

Pineapple with Yogurt and Mustard Sauce

Pineapple Pachadi

This deliciously different curry combines the raw pungency of mustard and the sweetness of pineapple. Try this recipe with other ingredients—chopped tomato for a Tomato Pachadi; or diced carrots and beans for a Vegetable Pachadi. Do not re-heat this dish; serve at room temperature with rice, cooked mung beans, and accompaniments.

In a medium saucepan, cook the pineapple in the ½ cup of water with the salt for 2 to 4 minutes, until the water has evaporated.

Add the coconut paste to the cooked pineapple and cook for 2 more minutes. Set aside to cool, then add the yogurt and stir lightly.

Heat the oil in a small skillet and add the mustard seeds. When they burst, add the shallots and sauté until they are lightly browned. Add the red chillis and curry leaves, stir, and remove from heat as soon as the chillis change color. Pour over the pineapple mixture.

Serves 4

2 cups ½-inch cubes pineapple
½ cup water
1 teaspoon salt
1 cup plain yogurt, lightly beaten
2 teaspoons oil
1 teaspoon mustard seeds
6 shallots, sliced
3 red chillis, halved
6 curry leaves

COCONUT PASTE

Grind to a fine paste:
1 cup grated fresh coconut
1 green chilli
1 teaspoon cumin seeds
½ teaspoon ground turmeric
1 teaspoon mustard seeds

VARIATIONS: Pachadi is made with a combination of yogurt and a vegetable or fruit. So you can also use other vegetables and fruits like cooked or sauteed brinjal, potatoes, green beans, or tomatoes.

Mango and Yogurt Curry

Kaalen

This is a tart, mildly spiced dish with unripe green mangoes in a yogurt and coconut gravy. Do not reheat this dish; serve with rice and accompaniments.

In a medium pan, cook the mango pieces with the green chillis, water, and salt for 3 to 5 minutes, until all the water has evaporated. Set aside.

Heat the oil in a small skillet and add the mustard seeds. When they burst, add the fenugreek, curry leaves, and red chillis.

Add the coconut paste and sauté for 1 minute over low heat, stirring continuously, so the mixture does not brown.

Add the cooked mangoes and yogurt. Keep stirring over low heat to prevent curdling for 2 to 3 minutes, until the gravy becomes thick. Remove from heat and continue to stir until the *kaalen* cools.

Serves 4

1 cup ½-inch cubes peeled green mangoes
4 green chillis, slit
½ cup water
1 teaspoon salt
2 tablespoons oil
1 teaspoon mustard seeds
¼ teaspoon ground fenugreek
6 curry leaves
3 red chillis, halved
4 cups plain yogurt, lightly beaten

COCONUT PASTE

Grind to a fine paste:
1 cup grated fresh coconut
1 pinch cumin seeds
½ teaspoon chilli powder
¼ teaspoon ground turmeric

Ripe Mango Curry

Pazha Manga Karri

Whole, sweet mangoes are simmered in a coconut milk gravy and lightly seasoned with mustard and chilli. Serve with rice, sautéed string beans, and accompaniments.

Put the whole mangoes in a pot with the thin coconut milk, shallots, green chillis, ginger, cumin, and salt and simmer over low heat for 10 minutes.

Add the thick coconut milk, remove from the heat and set aside to cool.

Heat the oil in a small skillet and add the mustard seeds. When they burst, add the curry leaves and red chillis. When the chillis turn a deep red (in about 5 seconds) pour over the curry.

Serves 4

4 ripe mangoes, peeled
2 cups thin coconut milk
8 shallots, sliced
4 green chillis, slit
½ teaspoon slivered fresh ginger
½ teaspoon ground cumin
1 teaspoon salt
½ cup thick coconut milk
1 teaspoon oil
1 teaspoon mustard seeds
6 curry leaves
2 red chillis, halved

Mung Beans, Cooked and Seasoned

Cherupayaru Olathiathu

Wholesome mung beans are cooked to a soft mush and seasoned with crushed spices. Red cowpeas can also be cooked in this way. Serve with rice, spiced buttermilk, and accompaniments, or with kanji and pappadams.

Serves 4

In a large pot, cook the mung beans with the 6 cups water and salt for 25 to 30 minutes, until soft and slightly mushy. Add more water if needed.

Using a mortar and pestle, combine and coarsely crush the red chillis, shallots, garlic, and pepper.

Heat the oil in a medium skillet and add the mustard seeds. When they burst, add the curry leaves and sauté for 1 minute. Add the crushed ingredients and fry for 2 minutes or until the shallots are lightly browned.

Add the cooked mung beans and keep stirring until almost dry.

2 cups dried mung beans, pre-soaked in warm water for 3 hours
6 cups water
½ teaspoon salt
2 red chillis
10 shallots
6 cloves garlic, in skin
¼ teaspoon ground pepper
2 teaspoons oil
1 teaspoon mustard seeds
6 curry leaves

Lentils with Coconut Milk

Parippu

This is the Malayali version of the ubiquitous lentil dish pre-pared all over India. This dish is best made with split pigeon peas, but can also be made with other lentils. Serve this creamy lentil curry in a Kerala vegetarian meal, along with rice, pineapple pachady, thiyal, *and crisp fried* pappadams.

In a large pot, cook the soaked peas with the water, thin coconut milk, salt, ginger, green chillis, turmeric, and cumin for 15 minutes. (The lentils should be soft and mushy.) Add the thick coconut milk and remove from the heat.

Heat the oil in a small skillet and add the mustard seeds. When they burst, add the shallots and garlic and fry for 1 minute until they are lightly browned. Add the curry leaves and red chillis and fry for a few seconds until the chillis turn a deep red. Pour into the cooked peas and stir.

NOTE: When reheating, do not let the lentils boil.

Serves 4

1½ cups dried split pigeon peas, pre-soaked in water for 2 hours; or dried lentils, pre-soaked for 1 hour, drained*
3 cups water
1 cup thin coconut milk
½ teaspoon salt
½ teaspoon sliced fresh ginger
3 green chillis, slit
½ teaspoon ground turmeric
½ teaspoon roasted ground cumin
½ cup thick coconut milk
1 tablespoon oil
½ teaspoon mustard seeds
¼ cup sliced shallots
3 cloves garlic, sliced
6 curry leaves
2 red chillis, torn in half

*NOTE: Any type of lentils or a combination of lentils can be used for this recipe.

Curried Chickpeas

Kadala Karri

The smaller native variety of chickpeas is preferred for this spicy chickpea curry. Hard and brown with a thick outer skin, they have to be pre-soaked overnight or longer before they can be cooked. The larger garbanzo beans or chickpeas can be used if the brown chickpeas are unavailable. Traditionally served as an accompaniment to puttu, *it can also be served with rice,* vegetable thorans, *and accompaniments.*

Dry roast the coconut in a heavy skillet over medium heat, stirring continuously until lightly toasted and browned. With a mortar and pestle or food processor, grind the toasted coconut with the peppercorns and ½ cup of water to a coarse paste. Set aside.

Heat the oil in a deep pot and add the mustard seeds. When they burst, add the onions and fry 1 to 2 minutes, until soft and transparent.

Add the green chillis, curry leaves, and ginger and garlic pastes and fry for 1 minute, then add the chopped tomatoes. Stir-fry for 1 more minute, until the tomatoes are soft. Add the chilli powder, coriander, and turmeric and stir-fry until the oil rises to the top.

Add the ground coconut paste and continue stirring for 1 to 2 minutes.

Add the water, salt, and soaked chickpeas. Stir, cover with a lid, and simmer for 30 to 40 minutes, until the gravy has thickened and the chickpeas are tender.

Serves 4

½ cup grated fresh coconut
6 whole peppercorns
3 tablespoons oil
½ teaspoon mustard seeds
1 large onion, sliced
2 green chillis, slit
6 curry leaves
1 teaspoon ginger paste
1 teaspoon garlic paste
½ cup chopped tomato
1 teaspoon chilli powder
1 tablespoon ground coriander
½ teaspoon ground turmeric
6 to 8 cups water
1 teaspoon salt
1½ cups dried chickpeas, pre-soaked in water overnight

Jackfruit Curry

Chakkapazham Karri

Jackfruit is the new superfood, packed with nutrients and flavor. It can be used when still unripe as a vegetable, and once ripe as fruit. The unripe flesh of the jackfruit is extremely versatile, and as it has the texture of meat, and so can be used as a nutritious substitute. Here it is made into a curry along with a few jackfruit seeds for additional flavor and texture. Serve with rice and a sautéed vegetable.

Put the jackfruit cubes along with the peeled seeds in a vessel with the water, salt, and turmeric.

Toast the coconut in a pan, stirring continuously till it turns light brown. When it has cooled down, puree with just enough water to make a smooth paste.

Heat the coconut oil in a medium-sized pot and add the mustard seeds. When they burst, add the shallots and fry till they turn translucent. Add the curry leaves and green chilli, and saute for 1 minute. Add the ginger paste and garlic paste and continue frying for another minute. Add the ground coriander seeds, ground fennel seeds, chilli powder, and lastly the asafoetida, and sauté over low heat till the oil rises to the surface. Now add the coconut puree and cook till the oil separates again.

Remove the jackfruit cubes and seeds from the water, and add them to the spice mix in the pot. Stir for a few minutes till they are coated with the mix. Add the tamarind paste, the reserved water, and salt if needed. Cook over low heat for around 10 minutes or until the jackfruit is tender.

Serves 4

500 grams (about 1 pound) unripe jackfruit, cut into 1-inch cubes*
6 jackfruit seeds, peeled and quartered
4 cups water
1 teaspoon salt
¼ teaspoon ground turmeric
½ cup grated fresh coconut
2 tablespoons coconut oil
1 teaspoon mustard seeds
¼ cup sliced shallots
8 curry leaves
1 green chilli, finely chopped
1 teaspoon ginger paste
1 teaspoon garlic paste
1 tablespoon ground coriander seeds
½ teaspoon ground fennel seeds
½ teaspoon chilli powder
¼ teaspoon asafoetida
1 tablespoon tamarind paste

*NOTE: To prepare the jackfruit first apply some oil on your palms, knife, and chopping board. Slice away the skin of the jackfruit and then remove the seeds and chop the jackfruit pulp into 1-inch cubes.

SEAFOOD AND RIVER FISH

Fringed by the Indian Ocean on the west, and blessed by a vast network of backwaters, lagoons, lakes and rivers, Kerala has a plentiful supply of a variety of fish. Seer fish, pomfret, mullet, shrimps, crabs, lobsters, mussels, clams, and oysters abound in the sea; a range of freshwater fish such as the prized karimeen (pearl spot), and shellfish like freshwater konju (lobster) thrive in the lagoons. Consequently, seafood features in the daily diet of most Malayalis.

Syrian Christians have concocted many unique and delectable recipes to prepare this fresh fare. Tiny sardines are marinated in spices and fried crisp in coconut oil; chunks of kaalanji (a backwater salmon) simmer with chilli and coccum in earthenware pots over smoky wood fires; whole karimeen is wrapped in banana leaves and roasted in the glowing embers of the hearth; and shrimps are stir-fried with slices of tender coconut, spices, and the omnipresent curry leaves.

The best of numerous seafood recipes are presented in this chapter, each with a unique combination of ingredients and cooking techniques. Most recipes can be interchanged—you can use the fish molee recipe to prepare a shrimp molee, or prepare crab cutlets using the recipe for fish cutlets.

Though coconut oil is the preferred cooking medium for most seafood dishes in Kerala, any other cooking oil can be used, with a teaspoon of coconut oil drizzled in for that distinctive flavor of South India.

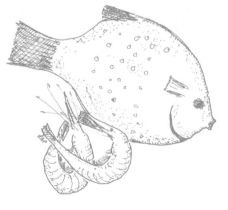

Seafood with a Slice of History

"You buy, we cook," declares the sign atop a row of fish stalls by the old boat jetty in Fort Kochi. We—my husband George and our children—are here on a gastronomic expedition, to sample the fresh seafood that is being hauled in even as we take our seats at the long wooden tables in this makeshift café. The fish stalls that line the shore are right by the cantilevered Chinese fishing nets which lower into the water and lift as we watch, fascinated. The catch is brought dripping with seaweed over to the fish stall and arranged on the counter for display. This is as fresh as it gets. We walk over to select our choice of fish.

We decide on a six-pound seer, a mound of large shrimps, four lobsters, and a plate of squid for starters. While we wait for the food, a vendor brings over tender coconut, expertly lops off the top and inserts plastic straws for us to sip the sweet water. When we are done, the shell is split open and he hands us a wedge of it so we can scoop out the soft, gelatinous flesh of the coconut.

The food is brought over in courses, starting with the squid, lobster, and a sliced green salad. The spicy rounds of squid that melt in the mouth are unlike the chewy lumps I have eaten previously, and the lobster—glistening with chilli, pepper, and its own juices—is succulent. Next comes the fried seer fish, cooked to perfection with just the right blend of spices, over which we squeeze fresh lime juice. The shrimps have been quickly sautéed with crushed spices in a large *cheena chatti,* sealing in the flavor that explodes in our mouths as we bite in. A large platter of red parboiled rice and a jug of spiced buttermilk are also served.

We notice the fishermen helping themselves to mounds of mashed tapioca from a large *kalam* and to sardine curry from the earthenware pot simmering in the back of the stall. Of course, we have to sample some and find it to be excellent. The not-so-secret formula of this feast is evident—fresh seafood, minimally spiced and briskly sautéed over a hot fire to sear and seal in its flavor. We pause to remember the complex history of this place.

Undoubtedly, Fort Kochi is culturally the richest part of Kerala; history lurks around every corner along with the heady fragrance of spices and the salt air. After lunch, we stroll past old colonial bungalows, churches, and monuments, reminded of early travelers who journeyed to these shores for a multitude of reasons, changing the character of this region forever.

Greek and Arab merchants were the first to arrive in dhows to trade for spices, followed by the Chinese in their magnificent ships. The Jews fled from their homeland to escape persecution and settled here, building a synagogue in what is now known as Jew Town. The Portuguese were the next to

Seafood restaurant at Fort Cochin

arrive with a fleet of ships, staying on to build a settlement that still survives as the present-day Fort Kochi. The Dutch traders followed suit, ousting the Portuguese from their position of power but leaving little to remember them by except the old Dutch cemetery and, we must concede, the *paalappam* or lace-rimmed pancake inspired by the Dutch pancake. The English, well-established in the rest of India, moved in with the might of the British Empire behind them, building docks, warehouses, the first business houses, and railways.

That evening, as the light begins to fade, casting spectacular shadows on the Chinese fishing nets by the wharf, we attend the Christmas vespers at St. Francis Church, built in A.D. 1500. We stop at Vasco da Gama's tomb and mingle with the locals of the area—a small community of Portuguese descent. Later, we are invited to a friend's house for an early supper of mutton stew with rice flour dumplings. We sip our wine and nibble on coconut sweets while our hosts prepare for midnight mass.

The next morning, after a lavish English breakfast at the Cochin Club, we head for Jew Town. The old spice warehouses that stretch back from the street to the open waters have now been converted to antique shops. It was here that the Jewish community once prospered, merchants and spice traders who built tall houses with inner courtyards. Until a few decades ago, they would sit on benches under the street lights playing canasta. The Jewish community has now dwindled to a handful of residents—keepers of the synagogue at the end of the street. Salman Rushdie, a recent traveller, walked these streets to capture the essence of this ancient land for his book, *The Moor's Last Sigh*.

Past the elaborately Gothic-styled Basilica of Santa Cruz and the old boatyards where warships and merchant vessels were once built for Arab merchants and the British navy, we stopped at the little Coonen Kurisu chapel, the chapel of the Bent Cross. History was made here in 1653 when an angry mob of Syrian Christians renounced the authority and oppression of the Portuguese and swore their allegiance to the Syrian Church. As the crowd of 1,000 gathered, the cross was tilted and numerous long ropes tied, so each person could be connected to it as they took the oath. The Syrian Church was now divided into the Syrian Catholics (*Pazhaya koor*) who stayed with the Roman Church and the Jacobites (*Puthen koor*) who owed their allegiance to the Patriarch of Antioch. Later, the Jacobites split into the Marthomites of the Anglican Church and the Church of the East, who followed the Nestorian patriarch, as well as several other factions.

Sated with good food and history, we stroll over to the wharf where a *jhunker* is just pulling in, chock full of cars, auto rickshaws, cyclists, and pedestrians. The wooden ferry raft is attached to a motorized boat that chugs its way to the numerous islands in this area. "Mattanchery, Vypeen, Willingdon Island," the boat man announces.

A jhunker

Fried Fish

Meen Varathathu

The marinade of spices featured in this recipe can be used to prepare any fish—slices of seer fish, red snapper, or sole, or smaller fish such as sardines and mackerel. If using large or whole fish, make shallow gashes in them and marinate, ensuring that the spices get into the slits and flavor the fish.

Coconut oil is the perfect cooking medium for fried fish, but any other oil can be used. The amount of oil can be varied according to preference, and the fish can be shallow-fried or deep-fried. If you prefer your fish grilled, add a tablespoon of oil to the spice marinade and grill as usual.

Serve with rice, spiced buttermilk, and a vegetable thoran.

Wash the fish and drain in a colander for 15 minutes.

Make a paste of the chilli powder, turmeric, peppercorns, and ginger and garlic pastes. Add the salt and lime juice and rub the mixture on the fish. Marinate for 1 hour.

Heat the oil in a skillet and fry a few pieces of fish at a time, over low heat. Flip over after 2 minutes when one side is done, and fry on the other side. Drain on paper towels.

Serves 4

2 pounds fish fillets, cut into small portions
1 tablespoon chilli powder
½ teaspoon ground turmeric
½ teaspoon crushed black peppercorns
½ teaspoon ginger paste
½ teaspoon garlic paste
1 teaspoon salt
1 teaspoon lime or lemon juice
½ cup oil for shallow-frying (or 3 cups if deep-frying)

Stuffed Fish Fry

Meen Nirachu Varathathu

Any whole fish can be used to prepare this dish, and then later be sliced into portions. Alternately, smaller fish can be used for individual servings. The stuffed fish is fried here but can also be grilled or broiled (see Note). Serve with a salad and chutney.

Clean the fish well and make a slit along one side for the stuffing. Make shallow gashes across the fish. Drain in a colander for 15 minutes.

PREPARE THE STUFFING:

With a mortar and pestle or food processor, grind the stuffing ingredients to a smooth paste.

PREPARE THE MARINADE:

Mix the chilli powder, turmeric, and peppercorns with the ginger and garlic pastes, lime juice, and salt.

Stuff the fish with the stuffing and seal shut with a toothpick. Rub the spice mixture all over both sides of the fish. Set aside for 1 hour.

Heat the oil in a large skillet and fry the fish over medium heat for 5 minutes or until it has browned evenly on both sides. Keep the skillet covered with a lid, to ensure that the fish cooks well.

NOTE: If you are grilling the fish, add a tablespoon of oil to the spice marinade.

Serves 4

4 (1 pound each) whole fish or 1 (3-pound) whole fish
1 cup oil for shallow-frying (or 6 cups oil for deep-frying)

STUFFING
½ cup fresh coriander (cilantro), coarsely chopped
½ cup grated coconut
1 green chilli
½ teaspoon lime juice
½ teaspoon salt

MARINADE
1 tablespoon chilli powder
½ teaspoon ground turmeric
½ teaspoon crushed black peppercorns
1 teaspoon ginger paste
1 teaspoon garlic paste
1 teaspoon lime or lemon juice
1 teaspoon salt

Fried Sardines with Backs Split

Mathi Muthuku Kuthi Varathathu

There is a sardine season in Kerala when the markets over-flow with the fish that Malayalis can never get enough of. These tasty favorites are simmered in curries, fried, steamed, or roasted. In this recipe, whole sardines with the scales left on are marinated in spices and fried crisp. Despite the gory title this dish goes by, sardine lovers agree that this is the best way to eat the fish. My cousin Rosie remembers eating sardines hot and crisp from the kitchen in Kanjirapally where over a hundred sardines were marinating in a large vessel as each batch was cooked. "A hundred!" we exclaimed, to which she replied "and more if there were guests." Of course, the best way to eat these would be at the kitchen table with a stack of paper napkins. Squeeze fresh lemon or lime juice on them as they emerge from the skillet, and peel off the scales as you eat.

Make a slit along the side of each sardine and remove the entrails from inside. Rub the sardines gently with a little salt and wash well. Drain in a colander for 10 minutes.

PREPARE THE SPICE MARINADE:

With a mortar and pestle or food processor, grind the marinade ingredients with a little water to make a smooth paste.

Mix the rice flour with the ground spice marinade. Rub the mixture over and inside the sardines. Set aside for 10 minutes.

Heat the oil in a deep skillet. Fry the sardines over medium heat in batches of four for 2 to 3 minutes, until they are crisp and brown.

Serves 2

12 whole sardines with scales left on
Salt
1 teaspoon rice flour
3 cups oil for deep-frying

SPICE MARINADE
6 shallots
1 (½-inch) piece ginger
4 cloves garlic
8 whole red chillis
1 teaspoon ground turmeric
1 teaspoon whole black peppercorns
1 teaspoon coarse sea salt

Fish Roasted in Banana Leaves
Meen Pollichathu

This classic fish preparation can be used to prepare any whole fish, but it somehow seems to have been created for the distinctive flavor of Kerala's most-favored fish: karimeen *(pearl spot). Indu Chandok, a friend and connoisseur of fine foods, once said that if a Malayali will share his* karimeen *with you, he must consider you a very dear friend indeed! However,* karimeen, *a freshwater fish indigenous to Kerala, is a somewhat acquired taste as it has a faintly brackish flavor. Also, apart from its large center bone, it has smaller, razor sharp ones. If you can get genuine* karimeen *at your local Indian grocery, live dangerously—this is something you could easily grow to love.*

There are different methods of preparing the spicy shallot paste for the marinade. In restaurants, the ingredients are fried and mixed with the fish. But this is the authentic method—slowly rubbing the shallots in oil, then gradually adding each ingredient until heat and friction do the trick. A heavy skillet can be substituted for the urali *it is traditionally prepared in. Banana leaves are used to line the base of the pan so that the fish can be turned over easily, but used as a wrapper here they seal in the flavors as well.*

Open the fish parcels and serve with a simple onion salad, to best savor the flavor of this delicious fish.

Serves 4

4 (1 pound each) whole fish, preferably *karimeen*
24 shallots, thinly sliced
2 tablespoons coconut oil, plus extra for oiling
    the skillet and the banana leaves
½ tablespoon crushed fresh ginger
1 tablespoon crushed garlic
10 curry leaves
2 green chillis, slit
1 teaspoon red chilli powder
1 teaspoon dried red chilli flakes
½ teaspoon ground turmeric
1 teaspoon vinegar
½ cup seeded and chopped tomato
1 teaspoon salt
4 large squares of banana leaves, wilted in hot
    water, for wrapping

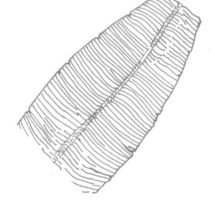

Clean and wash the fish and drain in a colander.

Put the shallots in a large mixing bowl. Add the coconut oil and gently pound the shallots with a wooden spoon or pestle until they turn transparent.

Add the ginger and garlic and continue rubbing, adding the curry leaves and green chillis, then the red chilli powder and flakes and the turmeric, pounding and blending after each addition. Finally, add the vinegar, tomato, and salt. When the mixture is well blended, rub the shallot mixture on each fish.

Grease the banana leaves lightly with coconut oil. Place a fish on each leaf and fold the leaves into neat parcels.

Coat the base of a large, heavy skillet with a spoonful of oil. Place the fish parcels in the pan, cover, and roast over low heat for 8 minutes. Turn the parcel over carefully when the leaf is brown and crisp, and cook for 5 more minutes.

Spiced Fish Roast
Meen Arapu Roast

*Any type of fish fillet or whole fish can be used for this recipe.
The fish is marinated with spices and slowly steam-roasted
with coconut milk in a heavy skillet with the lid shut tight.
It can also be baked or broiled in an oven.* Serve with hot rice
and side dishes or accompaniments.

Heat the oil in a small skillet and sauté the shallots
for 2 to 3 minutes, until light brown. Add the ginger and
garlic pastes and sauté for 1 minute. Add the chilli powder, turmeric, and peppercorns, and fry until the oil rises
to the top. Add the vinegar and salt.

Place the fish in a large heavy skillet and rub the fried
shallot mixture on both sides of the fish. Pour the coconut milk over the fish and cover the skillet with a
heavy lid. Cook over low heat for 10 minutes (20 minutes for whole fish).

When the fish is done and the coconut milk has been
absorbed by the fish, remove from the heat and set aside
for 15 minutes before serving.

Serves 6

¼ cup oil
1 cup sliced shallots
1 teaspoon ginger paste
1 tablespoon garlic paste
1 teaspoon chilli powder
½ teaspoon ground turmeric
½ teaspoon crushed black peppercorns
½ teaspoon vinegar
1 teaspoon salt
3 pounds skinless fish fillets, cut into large
   portions
1 cup thick coconut milk

Dried Fish Sauté

Onakka Meen Olathiathu

In Kerala, dried fish is a useful ingredient to have handy for those days when no other fish is available. It can be prepared in a matter of minutes—but make sure you soak the dried fish for a few hours before cooking, to remove its excess salt. Serve with rice and a yogurt-based dish such as spiced buttermilk *or* pachadi.

Heat the oil in a skillet, add the shallots and fry for 2 to 3 minutes, until light brown.

Add the green chillis, ginger, garlic, curry leaves, and tomato, and fry for 2 minutes. Add the chilli powder, turmeric, and peppercorns, and continue frying until the oil rises to the top.

Add the shredded fish to the pan. Continue frying, stirring occasionally, for 4 to 5 minutes, until the fish has mixed well with the spices and shallots.

Serves 2

1 tablespoon coconut oil
½ cup sliced shallots
2 green chillis, coarsely crushed
1 teaspoon grated fresh ginger
1 teaspoon crushed garlic
8 curry leaves
½ cup seeded and chopped tomato
1 teaspoon chilli powder
½ teaspoon ground turmeric
½ teaspoon crushed black peppercorns
1 cup dried fish, soaked in water for several
   hours, drained, and shredded

Fish Roe Sauté
Meen Mutta Olathiathu

My mother would use only fresh sardine roe for this simply prepared side dish, but any fresh roe can be used. As an alternative, try preparing this dish with a cup of grated fresh coconut instead of the beaten eggs. Serve on toast as a snack or as a side dish.

Heat the coconut oil in a skillet. Add the shallots and fry over low heat until they become transparent.

Add the ginger, curry leaves, and green chillis and continue to fry for a few minutes. Add the fish roe and salt and stir-fry for 3 to 5 minutes, until the roe crumbles and blends with the shallot mixture.

Pour the eggs into the pan and stir lightly. Cook for 2 minutes or until the eggs have set.

Serves 2 to 4

1 tablespoon coconut oil
¼ cup sliced shallots
¼ teaspoon crushed fresh ginger
6 curry leaves, chopped
2 green chillis, coarsely crushed
2 cups fresh sardine roe
½ teaspoon salt
2 eggs, beaten

Fish Cutlets
Meen Cutlets

This easy-to-prepare, crisply fried, spicy croquette can be made with any fresh flaked fish or even canned fish. Canned tuna or mackerel is the best and crabmeat or minced shrimps can also be used. For cocktail snacks, shape into smaller patties or balls and deep-fry until crisp and golden. You can also shallow-fry the cutlets with a minimum amount of oil. Serve with a salad, or stuff into a hamburger bun for a spicy fish burger.

In a medium bowl, combine all the ingredients except the egg, bread crumbs, and oil.

Shape the mixture into 12 round patties. Dip the patties in the beaten egg, coat with the bread crumbs, and set aside for 10 minutes.

Heat the oil in a skillet. Fry the cutlets for 2 minutes on each side, until crisp and brown.

Makes 12 small cutlets or
4 large burgers

4 cups cooked, flaked fish
1 cup coarsely mashed cooked potatoes
1 teaspoon chopped fresh mint
1 teaspoon chopped fresh coriander (cilantro)
¼ teaspoon minced fresh ginger
½ teaspoon minced green chilli
¼ teaspoon crushed black peppercorns
½ teaspoon salt
1 teaspoon lime or lemon juice
1 egg, beaten
½ cup dry bread crumbs
¼ cup oil, for shallow-frying

Yesterday's Fish Curry

Meen Vevichathu

This classic fish curry is simmered in an earthenware pot. It tastes best the day after it is prepared, and even better the next day—hence, it is often called "yesterday's fish curry." The sour, spicy fish curry will keep for a few days without refrigeration, and is one of the assortment of dishes prepared in advance for a wedding or family gathering. Any fleshy fish can be used for this recipe, and any deep vessel can be substituted for the earthenware one. Coccum—the sour fish tamarind that gives this fish curry its distinctive flavor—can be substituted with sour green mango slices.

There are many subtle variations to this dish, but this recipe, given to me by my dear friend Leela Oommen, is the best. The garlic paste and ground fenugreek are the secret to a nice, thick gravy, she informs me. She also uses the milder, brightly colored chilli powder from Kashmir for 'good color.' A retired obstetrician, she cheerfully lends a hand when she is often pressed back into service in our little town, dispensing useful tips on cooking and health care with equal enthusiasm.
Serve with rice and a vegetable thoran or mashed tapioca.

Heat the oil in a deep pot, add the sliced shallots and fry for 2 minutes. When they are lightly browned, add the ginger paste, garlic paste, and curry leaves and fry for 2 more minutes.

Lower the heat and add the spice paste and rice powder. Continue frying for 1 to 2 minutes, until the oil rises to the top.

Add the coccum, water, and salt, then add the fish and simmer for 10 minutes with the lid on. When the fish is cooked, drizzle the coconut oil over the curry.

Serves 4 to 6

¼ cup oil
8 shallots, thinly sliced
1 teaspoon ginger paste
2 tablespoons garlic paste
8 curry leaves
1 tablespoon rice powder
4 (2-inch) pieces coccum, soaked in water
2 cups water
2 tablespoons salt
2 pounds fish fillets, sliced into thick squares
1 teaspoon coconut oil (*optional*)

Spice Paste

Grind to a fine paste with a little water:
3 tablespoons Kashmir chilli powder
½ teaspoon ground turmeric
1 tablespoon ground coriander
½ teaspoon ground fenugreek, roasted

Fish Curry, Country-Style
Meen Vevichathu

This is the country-style version of Yesterday's Fish Curry (opposite page), and is standard fare at toddy shops along with mashed tapioca. This curry is often made with the head and tail of the fish—the bony pieces that remain from a whole fish, after the better cuts are taken for frying—and is also called mullum thala *(head and bones). The raw, unseasoned spices make this dish especially fiery, but it mellows as it is reheated over the next few days. In this recipe, the ingredients are mixed in a terracotta vessel or any deep pot and simmered until ready.* Serve with rice and sautéed red beans.

With a mortar and pestle or food processor, grind the chilli powder, turmeric, and fenugreek with a little water.

Put all the ingredients except the fish and oil into a deep terracotta vessel and mix well.

Add the fish and oil, cover, and simmer over low heat for 8 to 10 minutes, until cooked. (Do not mix the curry with a spoon; instead shake the vessel and swirl to mix so that the tender slices of fish do not break up.)

Uncover and let the dish cool. Once cool, cover and keep refrigerated for 1 day. Reheat and serve.

Serves 4 to 6

2 tablespoons chilli powder
½ teaspoon ground turmeric
½ teaspoon ground fenugreek, roasted
6 shallots, sliced
1 teaspoon sliced fresh ginger
8 cloves garlic, thinly sliced
8 curry leaves
4 (2-inch) pieces coccum, soaked in water
1 tablespoon salt
4 cups water
2 pounds fish pieces with bones
1 tablespoon coconut oil

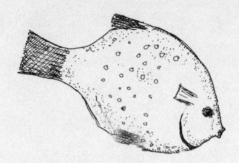

Fish Tales

My earliest memories of seafood stem from summer holidays in Kerala. We spent a considerable part of our vacation in Allepey, a small seaport with a long and once glorious association with the sea. My oldest sister, Shashi, lived there by the beach in a 150-year-old mansion, an early relic from the British Raj. When we visited her, mornings would see us rushing across to the shore where a fresh haul of fish had just been brought in. Fishing trawlers—country boats fitted with antiquated motors—returned daily from a night out at sea. The old lighthouse, whose beams once guided ships along this treacherous coast in the dead of night, now stood derelict. By the long wooden bridge that stretched for miles out to the sea, fishing nets were spread out to display the night's take and we shared the excitement of the moment with the tired but exultant fishermen. Like us, a crowd of early morning gawkers gathered to inspect the catch—a baby shark, a mound of tiny pink shrimps, an assortment of undeterminable fish, a stray octopus, and blobs of jellyfish, stingrays, mussels, and the prize catch of a good haul, seer fish.

Once, when the haul was meager, Shashi *chechi* made a bid for an entire catch, sight unseen. There was an element of surprise when we inspected the spoils back at home in her kitchen—a handful of shrimps to be sautéed with tender coconut, tiny *podi meen* (sprats) to be fried crisp, crabs, mussels for a spicy *olathu*, and a shimmering heap of multi-hued seashells that we stored away for our collection.

From Allepey, the narrow canals opened out to the vast labyrinthine backwaters of Kuttanad, home to an array of freshwater fish, shellfish, and crustaceans. Journeys through this waterworld were always associated with seafood and river fish—the spicy fish curry eaten at a little tea shop by the water's edge, the succulent *konju* lobster my sister once packed for the snakeboat races at Aranmula, and the roasted *karimeen* in banana leaf parcels at a family christening.

Fish Pappas
Meen Pappas

This is a rich, spice-laden fish curry with a coriander and co-coconut milk gravy. Slices of green mango can be substituted for the coccum for an interesting variation. Serve with rice and a vegetable thoran.

Heat the oil in a pot and add the mustard seeds. When they burst, add the fenugreek seeds, shallots, and curry leaves and fry until lightly browned.

Add the ginger, garlic, and green chillis, and fry for 1 to 2 minutes. Add the spice paste and fry until the oil rises and the spices are thoroughly sautéed.

Pour in the thin coconut milk, then add the coccum and salt. Add the fish pieces and simmer over low heat for 5 minutes.

Add the thick coconut milk (do not stir; instead, shake and swirl the curry to mix) and simmer for 5 minutes, until the gravy is thick.

Serves 4

2 tablespoons oil
1 teaspoon mustard seeds
½ teaspoon fenugreek seeds
12 shallots, sliced
8 curry leaves
1 teaspoon sliced fresh ginger
8 cloves garlic, thinly sliced
2 green chillis, slit
3 cups thin coconut milk
2 (2-inch) pieces coccum, soaked in water
1 teaspoon salt
1½ pounds fish with center bone, cut into thick slices
1 cup thick coconut milk

SPICE PASTE

Grind to a fine paste with a little water:
2 tablespoons ground coriander
1 teaspoon chilli powder
½ teaspoon ground turmeric
½ teaspoon ground black pepper

Fish Molee

Meen Molee

This creamy fish curry, probably influenced by travelers from Malaya, contains a delicate blend of spices and coconut milk. There are many variations of Fish Molee, with some recipes using tomatoes, turmeric, and other spices. This basic recipe is light and flavorful and uses just a few ingredients. Serve with paalappams or thick slices of bread.

Heat the oil in a wide, shallow pan.

Add the onions and fry until light brown; then add the ginger, garlic, green chillis, cloves, and curry leaves. Stir in the rice flour and continue to fry for 1 minute.

Add the thin coconut milk, vinegar, and salt; mix well. Add the fish, cover, and simmer for 10 minutes.

Add the thick coconut milk, and gently heat for 2 minutes. (Do not let it boil.)

Serves 4

2 tablespoons oil
2 onions, thinly sliced
1 tablespoon thinly sliced fresh ginger
8 cloves garlic, thinly sliced
3 long green chillis, slit
3 whole cloves
12 curry leaves
1 tablespoon rice flour or all-purpose flour
3 cups thin coconut milk
2 teaspoons vinegar
1 teaspoon salt
1½ pounds fish fillets, thickly sliced
1 cup thick coconut milk

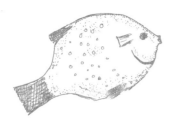

Fried Fish Molee

Varathu Meen Molee

This is a spicier version of the traditional Meen Molee (oppo-site page). It features pieces of fried fish simmered in a smooth, coconut milk gravy. Serve with rice and other accompaniments.

In a small bowl, mix together the chilli powder, turmeric and ½ teaspoon of the salt. Rub the fish with the spice marinade. Set aside for 1 hour.

Heat the oil in a wide, shallow pan, and fry the fish for 1 minute on each side. Remove the fish from the pan when lightly browned and set aside.

In the same oil, fry the onion for 2 to 3 minutes or until lightly browned. Add the ginger, garlic, green chillis, and curry leaves and sauté for 1 minute.

Add the tomato and stir in the rice flour. Stir in the thin coconut milk and remaining 1 teaspoon of salt.

Gently add the fried fish slices. Cook over low heat for 5 minutes. Gently stir in the thick coconut milk and simmer for another 5 minutes.

Sprinkle with fresh coriander just before serving.

Serves 4

1 teaspoon chilli powder
½ teaspoon ground turmeric
1½ teaspoons salt
1½ pounds fish fillets, thickly sliced
½ cup oil
1 onion, thinly sliced
1 tablespoon thinly sliced fresh ginger
10 cloves garlic, sliced
2 green chillis, thinly sliced
12 curry leaves
1 large tomato, quartered and seeded
1 tablespoon rice flour or all-purpose flour
2 cups thin coconut milk
½ cup thick coconut milk
1 tablespoon chopped fresh coriander (cilantro), for garnish

Fish and Mango Curry

Meenum Manga Karri

Thick slices of fish simmer in a smooth coconut puree with slices of green mango and spices to make a piquant fish curry. This recipe works well for shrimp as well. Serve with rice and a vegetable thoran.

Heat the oil in a pot, add the shallots and fry for 2 to 3 minutes, until they are lightly browned.

Add the fenugreek seeds and curry leaves and sauté for 1 minute. Add the coconut paste. Fry until the oil rises to the top, then add the water, fish, mango, and salt. Simmer over low heat for 5 minutes or until the fish is cooked.

Serves 2

2 tablespoons oil
½ cup sliced shallots
½ teaspoon fenugreek seeds
8 curry leaves
4 cups water
1 pound fish fillets, cut into thick slices
1 cup sliced sour green mango
1 teaspoon salt

COCONUT PASTE

Grind to a smooth paste:
1 cup grated fresh coconut
1 tablespoon chilli powder
1 teaspoon ground turmeric
2 green chillis
1 teaspoon chopped fresh ginger
8 cloves garlic, chopped
½ cup water

Fish with Grated Coconut

Meen Peera Pattichathu

This country-style fish preparation is made with any small fish such as sardines, mackerel, or even shrimp. Traditionally prepared in an earthen pot and tossed lightly, it is never stirred while cooking. Sliced green mangoes can be substituted for the coccum and are just as good. Serve with rice, plain buttermilk, and a vegetable side dish.

Coarsely crush the shallots, green chillis, fresh ginger, and garlic cloves using a mortar and pestle.

In a deep skillet mix the crushed shallot mixture, grated coconut, coccum, turmeric, water, and salt. Add the sardines and stir the mixture well to coat the fish.

Heat the coconut oil in a small skillet and add the curry leaves and red chillis. When the chillis turn dark red remove from the heat and pour into the fish. Shake the pot to mix the chilli mixture into the curry, do not stir with a spoon.

Cover the skillet and simmer for 8 to 10 minutes, until the water has almost evaporated. Set aside for 10 minutes before serving.

Serves 4

½ cup shallots, sliced
2 green chillis, slit
1 teaspoon sliced fresh ginger
6 cloves garlic, whole with skin
2 cups grated fresh coconut
3 (1-inch) pieces coccum, soaked in water
½ teaspoon ground turmeric
1 cup water
1 teaspoon salt
1 pound fresh sardines, cut in half
1 tablespoon coconut oil
8 curry leaves
2 red chillis, torn in half

Tomato Fish Curry

Thakali Chertha Meen Karri

One of my mother's recipes, this dish uses contemporary ingredients. The curry gets its sourness from tomato instead of the customary coccum, and uses onions instead of shallots. I call these items contemporary because my mother remembers a time when tomatoes and onions (called Bombay onions) were unheard of in Kerala. Serve with rice and accompaniments, or with crusty bread and a salad.

Heat the oil in a skillet. Add the onions and fry for 2 minutes or until soft and transparent.

Add the crushed garlic and ginger paste and fry lightly. Add the tomatoes and continue frying for a few minutes. Add the chilli powder and turmeric and fry until the oil rises to the top. Stir in the water and salt.

Put the fish slices into the tomato mixture and simmer over low heat for 5 to 8 minutes, until the fish is cooked. Remove the pan from the heat and add the lime juice and chopped coriander leaves while the curry is still hot. Cover the skillet and let the mixture sit for a few minutes so the curry can absorb the flavors of the lime and fresh herbs.

Serves 2

¼ cup oil
2 large onions, thinly sliced
2 tablespoons crushed fresh garlic
1 teaspoon ginger paste
2 cups seeded and chopped tomatoes
1 tablespoon chilli powder
½ teaspoon ground turmeric
2 cups water
1 teaspoon salt
1 pound fish with center bone, cut into thick slices
1 teaspoon lime juice
¼ cup coriander leaves (cilantro), chopped

Crushed Spice Fish Curry

Arapu Chathachathe Meen Karri

This recipe is usually used for sardines and mackerel, but also works well with larger cuts of fish. Coarse sea salt is traditionally used for most fish recipes in Kerala, and works well with this recipe. Serve with rice and accompaniments.

With a mortar and pestle or food processor, grind the sea salt, red chillis, chilli powder, and turmeric into a coarse paste. Mix the fish with the crushed chilli paste and place in a skillet.

With a mortar and pestle or food processor, grind the shallots, ginger, garlic, curry leaves, and coconut oil into a coarse paste. Add the crushed shallot mixture to the fish, along with the coccum and water.

Cover with a heavy lid and simmer for 8 to 10 minutes (depending on the fish used). The gravy will be thin and flecked with the crushed spices.

Serves 4

1 tablespoon coarse sea salt
6 whole red chillis
1 teaspoon chilli powder
½ teaspoon ground turmeric
1 pound sardines or sliced fish
½ cup shallots, sliced
1 teaspoon sliced fresh ginger
6 cloves garlic
6 curry leaves
2 tablespoons coconut oil
2 pieces (2-inch) coccum, soaked and torn in small pieces
2 cups water

Shrimp Fry
Chemmeen Olathiathu

A Syrian Christian classic, this dish can be simmered and stir-fried until dry, or cooked briefly until it is left with a thick gravy. The coconut pieces absorb the flavor of the shrimps and should not be omitted, likewise the coconut oil, if possible. This recipe (omitting the coconut pieces) is also used for konju—the delicious lobster from the backwaters of Kerala.

Serve with rice, spiced buttermilk and a vegetable thoran. I have also served it on toast for breakfast, and in canapés as cocktail snacks, minus the coccum, of course.

Put all the ingredients, except the oil, shallots, and garlic in a medium pot. Cook for 5 minutes over low heat, until almost all the water has evaporated and the shrimp are coated with the thick spice mixture.

Heat the oil in a medium skillet and fry the shallots and garlic until soft.

Add the cooked shrimp to this mixture, and stir-fry over low heat for 5 to 8 minutes, until the spiced shrimp are well fried.

Serves 3 to 4

1 pound medium or large shrimp, shelled and deveined
1 cup tender coconut pieces (*optional*)
2 tablespoons chilli powder
1 teaspoon ground turmeric
½ teaspoon crushed black peppercorns
8 curry leaves
1 teaspoon sliced fresh ginger
1 cup water
3 (2-inch) pieces coccum, soaked in water
1 teaspoon salt
5 tablespoons coconut oil
12 shallots, sliced
6 cloves garlic, sliced

Shrimp and Tomato Fry

Chemmeenum Thakali Olathiathu

A quickly prepared dish with tomatoes and ginger and garlic pastes, this requires no water. The shrimp simmer in their own juices and absorb the flavors of the ingredients. Serve with rice, vegetables, and lentils cooked in coconut milk.

Heat the oil in a skillet, add the shallots and fry for 1 minute.

Add the ginger paste, garlic paste, and tomatoes and continue cooking for 2 to 3 minutes, until lightly browned.

Add the chilli powder and turmeric, and fry until the oil rises to the top.

Add the shrimp and salt and briskly sauté over high heat for 5 minutes, until the shrimp are cooked and well coated with the tomato mixture. Sprinkle the ground cardamom, cinnamon, and cloves over the shrimp, stir, and remove from the heat.

Stir in the lime juice and chopped coriander leaves just before serving.

Serves 3 to 4

2 tablespoons oil
12 shallots, sliced
1 tablespoon ginger paste
2 tablespoons garlic paste
4 tomatoes, seeded and chopped
1 teaspoon chilli powder
½ teaspoon ground turmeric
1 pound medium shrimp, shelled and deveined
1 teaspoon salt
½ teaspoon ground cardamom
½ teaspoon ground cinnamon
½ teaspoon ground cloves
1 tablespoon lime juice
3 tablespoons chopped fresh coriander leaves (cilantro) for garnish

Shrimp in Ground Coconut Curry

Thenga Arache Chemmeen Karri

Ammini, the masseuse who cared for me and my daughters, gave me this easy country-style recipe for shrimp curry. In the original recipe, all the ingredients are mixed in an earthenware chatti *and simmered until the shrimp are cooked. However, I prefer this method of frying the ingredients in stages.*

Ammini's little house on the outskirts of Allepey town had a tiny stream meandering past her yard. Every morning, her son would spread a loosely woven cloth in the shallow water and scoop it up. Sometimes it opened to reveal a mound of soft sand but more often, a handful of tiny shrimp, sprats, or shellfish appeared. These she would toss in an earthenware pot with spices for a curry or simmer with grated coconut. As coccum was too expensive for everyday use, she would use raw mango or sour chillimbikka *(a sour, gherkin-like fruit) from the tree in her yard.*

Heat the oil in a deep skillet and fry the shallots and curry leaves for 1 minute. Add the coconut paste and fry until the oil rises to the top. Add the shrimp and fry for 5 minutes.

Add the water, coccum, and salt and cook over low heat for 8 to 10 minutes, until the shrimp are cooked and the gravy has thickened.

Serves 4

1 tablespoon oil
6 shallots, sliced
6 curry leaves
1 pound small or medium shrimp, shelled and deveined
3 cups water
2 pieces (2-inch) coccum, torn in half
1 teaspoon salt

COCONUT PASTE

Grind to a fine paste with a little water:
¼ cup grated fresh coconut
2 teaspoons chilli powder
½ teaspoon ground turmeric
1 teaspoon ground coriander
4 shallots
1 teaspoon chopped fresh ginger
6 cloves garlic

Dried Shrimp and Drumstick Bean Curry

Onakka Chemmeenum Muringakka Karri

*Drumstick beans (*moringa oleifera*) are long green beans resembling, of course, drumsticks. This is a deliciously simple preparation if you can find fresh drumstick beans at your local Indian grocer. Serve with rice, a vegetable* thoran, *and roasted* pappadams.

In a medium pot, cook the drumstick beans with the thin coconut milk and salt for 5 minutes or until the liquid is reduced by half. Set aside.

Heat the oil in a deep pot, and fry the shallots for 1 minute until soft. Add the ginger, garlic, and green chillis. Stir and add the tomatoes and curry leaves and continue frying for 2 more minutes.

Add the shrimp and rice flour and fry for 2 minutes, until well blended with the shallots.

Add the drumstick beans with their coconut milk gravy and simmer for 5 minutes.

Add the thick coconut milk and simmer over low heat for 2 minutes.

Serves 2

3 drumstick beans, cut into 2-inch pieces
6 cups thin coconut milk
1 teaspoon salt
1 tablespoon oil
8 shallots, sliced
1 teaspoon sliced fresh ginger
3 cloves garlic, sliced
2 green chillis, slit
2 tomatoes, chopped
6 curry leaves
1 cup dried shrimp
1 teaspoon rice flour
1 cup thick coconut milk

Crab Curry

Njandu Karri

This curry from the Malabar region of Kerala uses whole cleaned crabs but it can also be made with lump crabmeat. Serve with rice and accompaniments.

Heat the oil in a large lidded pot and add the shallots and sauté for 2 to 3 minutes, until they brown.

Add the curry leaves, ginger paste, and garlic paste and continue frying for a few minutes. Add the ground coriander and turmeric and fry for 1 minute.

Add the coconut paste and continue frying until the oil floats on top.

Add the crabs and sauté for 5 minutes, until the crabs are coated with the spice mixture. Add the water, salt, and coccum and simmer, covered, for 10 minutes.

Serves 2 to 4

2 tablespoons oil
8 shallots, sliced
8 curry leaves
1 tablespoon ginger paste
1 tablespoon garlic paste
2 tablespoons ground coriander
½ teaspoon ground turmeric
2 pounds fresh crabs, cleaned and halved
6 cups water
1 teaspoon salt
2 pieces coccum, torn in half

COCONUT PASTE

Grind to a fine paste with a little water:
½ cup grated fresh coconut
¼ cup fresh coriander leaves (cilantro)
3 green chillis
½ teaspoon ground cumin

Crab Fry

Njandu Pattichathu Olathiathu

A family favorite, this is a perfect picnic food. I sometimes add a cup of coconut milk as the crabs are sautéed to get a thick gravy to mop up with bread. Do not make Crab Fry if you have a plane to catch—you need time (and a stack of paper napkins) to really savor this dish. This recipe can also be used for crabmeat. Serve with a salad and crusty bread.

Put the crabs in a large pot with the chilli powder, coriander, turmeric, pepper, ginger, water, salt, and coccum. Mix well, cover, and simmer over medium heat for 8 to 10 minutes, until only 1 cup of liquid remains. Set aside.

In a large skillet, heat the oil and fry the onions for 2 minutes. Add the garlic and curry leaves and continue frying until the onions are lightly browned.

Add the cooked crabs along with the liquid and sauté for 10 to 15 minutes, until the spice mixture has dried to a thick paste and coated the crabs. Remove from heat.

NOTE: Add 1 cup of thick coconut milk if a gravy is required, stir and cook for 2 more minutes.

Serves 4

3 pounds large crabs in the shell, cleaned and cut into medium pieces
1 teaspoon chilli powder
2 tablespoons ground coriander
½ teaspoon ground turmeric
1 tablespoon crushed black peppercorns
1 teaspoon sliced fresh ginger
4 cups water
1 teaspoon salt
3 (2-inch) pieces coccum
¼ cup oil
2 onions, thinly sliced
6 cloves garlic, sliced
8 curry leaves

Spicy Mussel Fry
Kallumekka Olathiathu

Mussels need little cooking, and one way of preparing them would be to quickly stir-fry the mussels with all the ingredients. However, I prefer the following method, as the mussels absorb the spices during the first cooking, and the hot oil then seals in the flavor. Clams and other shellfish can also be cooked in this way. Serve with rice, parotta, or on toast as a snack.

Place the mussels in a pan with all the ingredients except the oil, shallots, garlic, and curry leaves. Cook for 4 to 5 minutes, until the water has almost completely evaporated but the mussels are still moist.

Heat the oil in a large skillet and fry the shallots until soft. Add the garlic and curry leaves and continue frying for 2 minutes, until they are lightly browned.

Pour the cooked mussels with liquid into the skillet and stir-fry over low heat for 5 minutes, until the mussels are coated with the spices.

Serves 4

1 pound mussels, cleaned and debearded
½ cup grated fresh coconut
1 tablespoon chilli powder
½ teaspoon ground turmeric
½ teaspoon crushed black peppercorns
½ teaspoon minced fresh ginger
1 cup water
1 teaspoon tamarind paste
1 teaspoon salt
1 tablespoon oil
12 shallots, sliced
4 cloves garlic, sliced
8 curry leaves

Sautéed Squid

Koonthal Varathathu

Squid turns rubbery if overcooked, so once marinated they must be quickly stir-fried and served hot, with a fresh sprinkling of lime juice. Serve with rice and accompaniments or as a snack.

Grind the garlic, chilli powder, turmeric, and peppercorns to a coarse paste in a mortar and pestle.

Mix the garlic paste with the rice flour, salt, and lemon juice and rub into the squid. Let the squid marinate in the spices for at least 2 hours at room temperature.

Heat the oil in a skillet and add the squid. Stir-fry over high heat for 3 to 5 minutes, removing from the heat when the spices brown.

Serves 2

2 cloves garlic, chopped
1 teaspoon red chilli powder
½ teaspoon ground turmeric
½ teaspoon crushed black peppercorns
1 teaspoon rice flour
1 teaspoon salt
2 teaspoons lime juice
½ pound squid, cut into ½-inch pieces, well
washed and drained
2 tablespoons oil

Preparing Beef Cutlets (page 112)

BEEF, MUTTON, AND PORK

Syrian Christians have many methods of preparing meats—they can be curried in spices and coconut milk, sautéed with tender bits of coconut, shaped into spicy cutlets and meatballs, or steam-roasted. In traditional homes, meat is served at every meal and it is not uncommon to find a dish of *erachi olathiathu* or sautéed meat and other leftover meats at the breakfast table, too.

Beef is the favored meat, with mutton (goat) coming a not so close second. Goat meat is preferred to lamb which is rarely used. Mutton is simmered in coconut milk with vegetables and spices for Kerala *ishtew* (stew) or curried and layered with rice for a biryani. Ground meat, usually beef, is a relatively new ingredient in Kerala cuisine that has been adapted to suit local tastes with a select blend of spices. Pork, which was introduced by the Portuguese, is served on special occasions like weddings, Christmas, or Easter where a spicy pork roast or vindaloo is featured. Wild game, liver, and dried meats are other favorites.

In Kerala, roasting is a popular method of cooking. It involves searing the meat with spices and oil, then allowing the meat to cook in its own juices; tougher meats require some water added at this stage. Roasting is best done in a large, heavy, bell metal vessel called an *urali* that retains heat for a long time. The *urali* is covered with a heavy lid on top of which coals are placed, creating an oven-like atmosphere within.

Today, the pressure cooker has become an invaluable cooking vessel for meats as the wood-fire hearth becomes redundant. Using the same cooking techniques, meats can be cooked in a fraction of the time it normally takes.

The recipes here have been adapted for the more tender cuts of meats available in the U.S. They can be used to prepare all kinds of meat and even poultry. For example, the Fried Meat recipe (page 106) can be used for pork or chicken and the Mutton Pepper Fry recipe (page 116) can be used for beef.

105

Fried Beef
Erachi Olathiathu

Erachi Olathiathu is a spicy fried meat made with beef or pork prepared in most Syrian Christian homes. Some like the meat fried crisp and hard, some prefer it soft with a thick gravy. Coconut oil complements the spiced meat perfectly, but any other oil can be substituted. The tender coconut pieces are optional. Serve with rice, spiced buttermilk, and a vegetable thoran. This dish can also be served as a side dish at a Kerala breakfast, with appams or puttu and ishtew.

Put the beef in a deep pot with the 3 cups of water and all the other ingredients except the coconut, oil, garlic, and shallots. Cook uncovered for 30 minutes over medium heat.

When the beef is cooked and tender, add the coconut and cook for 5 more minutes, until the water has almost evaporated.

Heat the oil in a heavy skillet and fry the garlic and shallots for 2 to 3 minutes or until light browned.

Add the cooked meat mixture and stir-fry over low heat for 8 to 10 minutes, until the meat is browned. If you prefer a softer consistency, add an additional ½ cup of water at this point and cook for 2 more minutes.

Serves 4

1 pound beef, cut into ¾-inch cubes
3 cups water
3 tablespoons ground coriander
1 teaspoon chilli powder
½ teaspoon ground turmeric
½ teaspoon crushed black peppercorns
2 green chillis, slit
1 small piece fresh ginger, cut into thin strips
12 curry leaves
1 teaspoon salt
1 teaspoon vinegar
1 cup fresh coconut pieces
¼ cup coconut oil
4 cloves garlic, sliced lengthwise
1 cup sliced shallots

Beef and Potato Curry

Mooriyerachi Karri

This curry can be made mild or spicy according to taste; if you want a creamier consistency, a cup of coconut milk can be added. Serve with rice and vegetables or puttu.

Serves 4

Heat the oil in a deep pot. Add the onions and fry for 1 to 2 minutes, until soft and transparent. Then add the green chillis, ginger paste, and garlic paste. Fry for 2 minutes, then add the tomatoes. Stir-fry for 2 more minutes, until tomatoes are soft.

Add the chilli powder, coriander, turmeric, cardamom, cinnamon, and cloves and stir-fry until the oil rises to the top.

Add the beef and salt and mix well, then stir in the water. Cover and cook over medium heat for 30 minutes or until the meat is almost cooked.

Add the potatoes and cook for 5 more minutes, until both the meat and potatoes are tender.

3 tablespoons oil
1 large onion, sliced
2 green chillis, slit
1 teaspoon ginger paste
1 teaspoon garlic paste
½ cup chopped tomato
1 teaspoon chilli powder
2 tablespoons ground coriander
½ teaspoon ground turmeric
½ teaspoon ground cardamom
¼ teaspoon ground cinnamon
¼ teaspoon ground cloves
1 pound beef, cut into ¾-inch cubes
1 tablespoon salt
8 cups water
2 large potatoes, cut into 1-inch cubes

Beef and Tapioca

Mooriyerachi Chertha Kappa Puzhakku

A meal in one, this is a simply prepared country-style dish popular among the Christians from Trichur, a small town near Kochi. It can also be prepared with curried pork, mutton, or lamb.

Serves 6

With a mortar and pestle or food processor, coarsely grind the coconut and ginger.

Put into a deep pot the cubed beef, 6 cups of the water, 1 tablespoon of the salt, the coriander, chilli powder, and turmeric. Cover and cook over low heat for 30 minutes or until the meat is tender and a little gravy remains.

In another pot, cook the tapioca in the remaining 6 cups of water with the remaining salt for 10 minutes. The tapioca should be soft but still firm. Drain, then stir in the coconut mixture. Set aside.

In a deep pot, heat the oil, add the shallots and fry for 2 minutes. Add the garlic and curry leaves and continue frying until lightly browned.

Add the cooked meat and sauté for 5 minutes or until the oil rises to the top. Mix the cooked tapioca with the beef, and cook over a low heat for 5 minutes, stirring continuously.

2 cups grated fresh coconut*
1 small piece fresh ginger, chopped
1 pound beef, cubed
12 cups water
2 tablespoons salt
2 tablespoons ground coriander
1 teaspoon chilli powder
½ teaspoon ground turmeric
1 pound fresh tapioca, cubed
3 tablespoons coconut oil
1 cup sliced shallots
6 cloves garlic, crushed
8 curry leaves

*NOTE: For a deeper flavor, dry roast the grated coconut in a skillet or oven until lightly browned before grinding.

Spicy Beef Pot Roast
Mooriyerachi Roast

A spiced-up version of a traditional recipe, this pot roast is best simmered on a back burner for three to four hours until tender. I got this recipe from an old estate journal. "Pot Roast was made when the Sayipu Pilots came to spray the estate. It was too spicy for them, so no chillis next time," it was recorded. In the remote rubber estates of Kerala, the arrival of special guests like the aerial spraying team (usually Westerners) who visited periodically demanded a blander menu. This is possibly one of the recipes of the Portuguese cook, Pacheek, duly recorded for these occasions.

Large quartered potatoes and thick rounds of carrots can be added toward the end of cooking, if desired. This pot roast can also be made in a large Dutch oven or broiled in the oven. However, the method of roasting given here imparts a moister flavor to the meat. Serve the sliced meat with the vegetables and thick slices of bread.

Place the meat in a large mixing bowl. Add the salt and flour to the spice paste and rub this all over the meat. Marinate the beef for 3 hours at room temperature.

Heat the oil in a large, heavy-bottomed pot. Add the shallots and meat, and brown the meat on all sides over low heat.

Add enough water to just cover the meat and simmer over low heat for 3 to 4 hours, adding the potatoes and carrots 20 minutes before the end of cooking.

When the meat is done and about 2 cups of gravy remains in the pan, remove the meat from the pan and let it sit for an hour before slicing. Set the gravy aside. When ready to serve, slice the meat. Reheat the gravy and pour it over the sliced meat. Serve with the carrots and potatoes.

Serves 6 to 8

3- to 4-pound whole beef round or rump roast, rinsed
2 tablespoons salt
3 tablespoons all-purpose flour
½ cup oil or beef suet
24 large peeled shallots
4 large potatoes, quartered
3 carrots, cut into thick rounds

SPICE PASTE

Grind to a fine paste:
3 tablespoons mustard seeds
5 red chillis
6 whole cloves
3 (1-inch) cinnamon sticks
2 tablespoons black peppercorns
8 cloves garlic
3 tablespoons vinegar

NOTE: To make this roast in an oven, remove the browned meat to a large roasting pan or baking dish and add 2 cups of water. Cover with foil and roast at 350 degrees F for 2 hours, basting occasionally with the liquid at the bottom of the pan. Add the potatoes and carrots, cover with foil, and cook for 30 more minutes. Remove from the oven and let it sit for an hour before slicing.

Chilli Beef Steaks
Molagu Chertha Mooriyerachi Chops

This recipe for steaks (called chops in India) spiced up with crushed red chillis is adapted from the original—one of the infamous Missy's recipes (pages 206). In India, beef is rarely tender and needs much preparation. A beef steak would have to be tenderized with raw papaya, pulverized with a mallet, or parboiled and then pan-fried. This method is for tender cuts that can be pan-fried, broiled, or grilled. I have often used the marinade for barbecued pork chops. Serve with bread and boiled vegetables.

In a mortar and pestle, grind the marinade ingredients into a thick paste. Rub this over the steaks and marinate at room temperature for 3 hours.

Heat the oil in a large skillet and fry the onion rings until they are golden brown. Remove them from the pan and set aside.

Fry the potatoes in the same oil until they are golden brown. Remove from the pan and set aside.

In the same skillet, sear the steaks on both sides and pan-fry for 12 to 15 minutes, until they are cooked as desired.

Serve the onion rings on top of each steak with the fried potatoes on the side.

Serves 4

4 thick steaks, about ½ pound each
½ cup oil
2 large onions, sliced into rings
2 large potatoes, sliced thick and parboiled

MARINADE:
1 teaspoon chilli powder
8 cloves garlic, crushed
1 teaspoon crushed black peppercorns
1 tablespoon tamarind paste
1 teaspoon jaggery or brown sugar
1 tablespoon salt

Ground Beef and Potato Fry

Kothiyerachiyum Kezhangu Olathiathu

This dry curried dish is made with ground beef or lamb. The potatoes are optional, and can be replaced by a cup of peas. Ground beef made its way into kitchens in Kerala quite recently, so this is a fairly new addition to the Syrian Christian kitchen. This dish can be served with rice or pathiri, *or on toast as a snack.*

Heat the oil in a skillet. Add the potatoes and fry until golden brown; remove from the pan and set aside.

In the same oil, fry the onion, ginger, and garlic for 2 minutes. Add the tomatoes, and fry for 2 more minutes. Add the coriander, chilli powder, turmeric, pepper, cinnamon, cloves, and cardamom, and fry over low heat until the oil rises to the top.

Add the ground beef and stir-fry for 5 minutes, until the spices and meat are blended together. Add the salt.

Add the 4 cups of water and cook, covered, for 10 minutes (if the beef is tender, you can omit this step and not add any water).

Add the potatoes and stir-fry until the meat is dry.

Remove from the heat, add the lime juice and coriander leaves and let sit covered for a few minutes before serving.

Serves 4

½ cup oil
2 large potatoes, cut into ½-inch cubes
1 large onion, chopped
1 teaspoon minced fresh ginger
8 cloves garlic, sliced
2 tomatoes, chopped
3 tablespoons ground coriander
2 teaspoons chilli powder
1 teaspoon ground turmeric
½ teaspoon finely ground black pepper
½ teaspoon ground cinnamon
½ teaspoon ground cloves
½ teaspoon ground cardamom
1 pound ground beef*
1 tablespoon salt
4 cups water
1 teaspoon lime juice
1 tablespoon chopped fresh coriander leaves
   (cilantro)

*VARIATION: This recipe can also be made with ground chicken or lamb.

Beef Cutlets

Mooriyerachi Cutlet

These spicy cutlets, also known as croquettes, can be shaped into small rounds for cocktail snacks or larger rounds for a spicy hamburger. An ideal party or picnic food, these cutlets are very versatile, and I often keep a stock of frozen cutlets for unexpected visitors.

In a medium skillet, cook the ground beef with the water, salt, chilli powder, and crushed peppercorns for 10 minutes, until the water has evaporated. Remove from heat and allow to cool.

When the meat has cooled, add the mashed potatoes and mix well. Add the onions, ginger, green chilli, coriander leaves, and lime juice. Mix well and shape into 2-inch round patties.

Place the beaten egg in a shallow bowl, and the bread crumbs in another bowl.

Dip each cutlet into the egg and coat with bread crumbs, so that each is evenly covered with the crumbs. Set aside for at least an hour.

Heat the oil in a skillet and fry the cutlets over medium heat until golden brown.

Makes 12 to 15 cutlets
or 4 large burgers

1 pound ground beef*
4 cups water
1 tablespoon salt
1 teaspoon chilli powder
½ teaspoon crushed black peppercorns
2 boiled potatoes, lightly mashed
1 cup finely chopped onions
1 tablespoon minced fresh ginger
2 teaspoons minced green chilli
¼ cup chopped coriander leaves (cilantro)
1 tablespoon lime juice
1 egg, beaten
½ cup fresh bread crumbs, toasted
Oil for frying

VARIATION: This recipe can also be made with ground chicken or lamb.

Meatball Curry

Kofta Karri

I like to add a cup of thick coconut milk to this toward the end of cooking, for a creamier curry. The meatballs can be made with ground beef or lamb. Like the beef cutlets, they can also be frozen and used for finger foods or picnics. Serve this curry with Kerala parotta or rice.

MAKE THE MEATBALLS:

In a medium bowl, mix all the ingredients for the meatballs and form into balls 1 inch in diameter. Set aside for an hour.

MAKE THE CASHEW PASTE:

With a mortar and pestle or food processor, grind to a fine paste the cashews, coriander leaves, mint, and green chillis.

Heat the oil in a deep pan and lightly fry the meatballs in batches of 5 for 2 minutes. As the meatballs are fried, drain on paper towels and set aside.

Fry the onion in the same oil for 2 minutes until soft. Add the tomatoes, ginger paste, and garlic paste and fry for 2 more minutes. Add the yogurt and cashew paste and stir-fry until the oil rises to the top.

Add the coriander, turmeric, cumin, cinnamon, cloves, and cardamom, and continue frying for 1 minute. When the oil rises to the top once more, add the water and salt.

Put the meatballs into the curry sauce and simmer over low heat for 10 minutes. Add the lime juice just before serving.

Serves 4

MEATBALLS

1 pound ground beef or lamb
2 eggs, beaten
½ tablespoon minced green chilli
½ tablespoon finely chopped coriander leaves (cilantro)
1 teaspoon salt

CASHEW PASTE

½ cup chopped cashews
¼ cup coriander leaves (cilantro)
1 tablespoon chopped fresh mint leaves
3 green chillis

½ cup oil
1 large onion, chopped
2 tomatoes, quartered
1 tablespoon ginger paste
2 tablespoons garlic paste
1 cup plain yogurt
2 tablespoons ground coriander
1 teaspoon ground turmeric
½ teaspoon ground cumin
½ teaspoon ground cinnamon
½ teaspoon ground cloves
½ teaspoon ground cardamom
6 cups water
1 tablespoon salt
1 tablespoon lime juice

Dried Beef Fry

Onakka Mooriyerachi Olathiathu

This is a simply prepared dish with sun-dried meat, onions, and spices. The meat must be soaked in water to soften, then shredded and pounded. Dried meat, whether beef or game, has an intense flavor as its essence becomes concentrated when the meat is sun-dried and smoked. Serve with rice and a yogurt-based dish.

Soak the dried beef pieces in water for 2 hours to soften and remove some of the salt.

Take the meat from the water and pound it with a mallet, shredding the meat into smaller pieces.

Heat the oil in a skillet, add the onions and fry until brown. Add the tomatoes, curry leaves, ginger, and garlic, and continue frying for 1 minute. Add the chilli powder, turmeric, and crushed peppercorns and sauté until the oil rises to the top.

Add the shredded meat and stir-fry over low heat for 5 minutes, until the meat is browned and coated with the onion mixture.

Serves 2

½ pound dried beef
2 tablespoons oil
2 onions, sliced
2 tomatoes, quartered
8 curry leaves
1 teaspoon minced fresh ginger
6 cloves garlic, sliced
1 teaspoon chilli powder
½ teaspoon ground turmeric
1 tablespoon crushed black peppercorns

Liver Fry

Karal Olathiathu

Any type of liver can be used for this recipe. However, if you are using chicken livers it is not necessary to steam the meat. Just sauté the tender slices of liver after marinating for half an hour. Serve as a side dish or a main meal. This dish can also be served on toast as a snack or breakfast dish.

Rub the livers with a little salt and turmeric, and steam for 5 minutes until firm. Slice into thin pieces.

Heat the oil in a heavy skillet and sauté the onion until golden brown. Add the garlic, green chillis, curry leaves, and tomato, and continue frying for 2 minutes.

Add the mustard powder and peppercorns and sauté over low heat for 1 minute. Add the sliced liver and more salt, if necessary, and continue frying until the liver is browned and coated with the onion and spice mix. Sprinkle with lime juice before serving.

Serves 4

1 pound calf's or chicken livers
1 teaspoon salt
1 teaspoon ground turmeric
3 tablespoons oil
1 large onion, sliced
6 cloves garlic, sliced
2 green chillis, slit
6 curry leaves
1 large tomato, chopped
1 teaspoon mustard powder
1 tablespoon coarsely crushed black
   peppercorns
½ teaspoon lime juice

Mutton Pepper Fry
Atterachiyum Kurumolagu Olathiathu

Lamb or mutton cubes are simmered here with coriander and chilli powder and then sautéed with cracked black peppercorns and curry leaves. This fry is especially delicious when cooked with coconut oil. Serve with fried potatoes, parotta, and a salad.

Serves 2 to 3

In a small, dry skillet, lightly toast the cardamom pods, cloves, and cinnamon stick. With a mortar and pestle or spice grinder, grind them to a powder.

In a medium pot, cook the mutton with the water, coriander, chilli powder, turmeric, and salt for 20 minutes, until the meat is tender and the water has almost evaporated, leaving just enough liquid to keep the meat moist.

Heat the oil in a heavy skillet and fry the onion until soft. Add the tomatoes, crushed garlic, and curry leaves and continue frying for 2 more minutes.

Add the cracked peppercorns and cooked mutton and sauté for a few minutes over low heat. Add the ground spices and fry the meat 4 to 5 minutes, until the spices have blended and the meat is browned.

3 cardamom pods
3 cloves
1 (1-inch) cinnamon stick
1 pound mutton (goat meat) or lamb, cubed
4 cups water
2 tablespoons ground coriander
1 teaspoon chilli powder
½ teaspoon ground turmeric
1 teaspoon salt
¼ cup oil
1 cup sliced onion
4 tomatoes, quartered
3 tablespoons crushed garlic
12 curry leaves
2 tablespoons cracked black peppercorns

Aunty's Curried Ribs

Ammai udey Varial Karri

My sister has this down in her recipe book as 'Kuzhikaate Ammai's Curried Ribs,' this being her famed specialty, but I have the same recipe down as 'Thresi Vellima's Curried Ribs.' Needless to say the two aunts were cousins and had possibly swapped recipes, but whoever they belong to, this is a delicious way to prepare short ribs. Serve with rice and accompaniments or with parotta.

Heat the oil in a large deep pot. Add the onions and fry for 1 to 2 minutes, until soft. Add the tomatoes and continue cooking for a few more minutes. Add the coriander, turmeric, and peppercorns and fry until the oil rises to the top.

Add the cardamom, cinnamon, and cloves, stir, and fry for 1 minute.

Add the coconut paste, short ribs, salt, and water and cook for 20 minutes over medium heat until the meat is tender. The water should have evaporated and the remaining gravy should be thick and coat the meat.

Heat the oil in a small skillet and add the mustard seeds. When they burst, add the shallots and curry leaves and fry until golden brown. Pour over the meat and stir to blend in.

Serves 2 to 3

¼ cup oil
1 cup sliced onions
2 tomatoes, seeded and quartered
2 tablespoons ground coriander
1 teaspoon ground turmeric
1 teaspoon crushed black peppercorns
3 cardamom pods, crushed
1 (1-inch) stick cinnamon, crushed
4 whole cloves
1 pound short ribs
1 tablespoon salt
4 cups water, or as needed
1 tablespoon coconut oil
1 teaspoon mustard seeds
6 shallots, thinly sliced
8 curry leaves

Coconut Paste

Grind to a coarse paste:
1 cup grated fresh coconut
4 green chillis
1 tablespoon chopped fresh ginger
2 tablespoons chopped fresh garlic
1 teaspoon cumin seeds

Pork Roast

Panniyerachi Roast

This dish is often prepared for weddings, Christmas, or Easter. Roasts are prepared in large uralis, *which retain a slow steady heat; covered with a heavy lid, they become an oven of sorts. As roasts are invariably cooked over a wood fire, they imbibe the wood smoke which gives the meat its unique flavor.*

My husband, George, comes from a family of serious food enthusiasts, and a pork roast prepared by master cook Verghese at a christening nearly thirty years ago is remembered to this day by all who were at the feast. Verghese is long deceased and unfortunately, the recipe has departed with him. On enquiry, I was told by many, "Yes, I remember the mustardy flavor ... the crisp, thin slices ... the perfectly spiced, tender meat ..." and so on. Finally, after much discussion, this is what I was able to reconstruct of the recipe. Serve as a main dish with sliced fried potatoes.

Mix the garlic and chilli paste, spice powder, and salt in a bowl. Rub this mixture all over the pork loin and set aside for 3 hours at room temperature.

Heat half the oil in a heavy cast-iron roasting pot, and sear the meat evenly on all sides. When the meat is browned, place the slices of pork fat on top of the meat. Cover and cook for 3 hours over low heat, sprinkling occasionally with a tablespoon of water.

Remove the meat from the pot and set aside to rest. Reserve the pan drippings in the pot, skimming off the extra fat after the drippings have cooled. When the roast has completely cooled, slice the pork into thin pieces.

Mix the reserved pan drippings with the flour and 3 cups of water. Heat the remaining ½ cup of oil in a heavy skillet and fry the onions until golden brown. Add the sliced pork to the onions, stirring constantly. When the pork slices have browned, add the drippings mixture. Cook until the gravy is dark and thick and has coated the sliced pork. Once again, skim off extra fat before serving.

Serves 8 to 10

1 tablespoon salt
5-pound boneless lean pork loin
1 cup oil
½ pound pork fat, thinly sliced
1 tablespoon all-purpose flour
3 cups water plus 1 cup for sprinkling
6 onions, sliced

GARLIC AND CHILLI PASTE

Grind to a fine paste:
1 cup chopped garlic
15 red chillis
½ cup shallots
½ cup mustard seeds
¼ cup fenugreek seeds
¼ cup chopped fresh ginger
2 tablespoons vinegar

SPICE POWDER

Grind to a powder:
1 tablespoon black peppercorns
12 whole cloves
8 cardamom pods
3 (1-inch) cinnamon sticks

NOTE: To make this roast in an oven, remove the browned meat to a large roasting pan, place the pork fat on top. Cover with foil and roast at 350 degrees F for 2 hours, sprinkling occasionally with a tablespoon of water.

Pork Vindaloo

Panniyerachi Vindaloo

Vindaloo, *a recipe borrowed from the Latin Christians of Portuguese descent, is a popular vinegary dish served on special occasions. Fatty pork is preferable, though lean pork can also be used. My mother would add cubes of fried potatoes towards the end of cooking which would absorb the rich flavor of the curry. When she made a beef vindaloo, she would also add a spoonful of sugar or powdered molasses to offset the sourness.*

Kashmir chilli powder is used in this recipe instead of the spicier South Indian chilli powder. Though less pungent, its bright red hues give the vindaloo its trademark color. Serve with rice and accompaniments, or with thick slices of fresh bread and a salad.

Heat the oil in a deep pot or large skillet. Add the pieces of pork and fry for 2 minutes, until they are lightly seared; remove from the pan and set aside.

In the same oil, fry the onions until soft. Add the tomatoes, garlic paste, and ginger paste, and fry for 1 minute or until the oil rises to the top. Lower the heat, add the mustard paste and fry for 1 minute. Add the chilli powder and turmeric and fry for 1 minute, stirring continuously. Add the spice powder and continue frying for 2 minutes or until the oil rises to the top again.

Pour the water into the pot and add the pork and salt. Simmer over low heat for 20 minutes or until the meat is cooked.

OPTIONAL: Add cubed fried potatoes 5 minutes before the end of cooking.

Serves 3 to 4

¼ cup oil
1 pound pork cubes
2 large onions, chopped
3 tomatoes, chopped
1 tablespoon garlic paste
2 teaspoons ginger paste
2 teaspoons Kashmir chilli powder
1 teaspoon ground turmeric
3 cups water
1 teaspoon salt

MUSTARD PASTE
Grind to a fine paste:
1 tablespoon mustard seeds
1 tablespoon vinegar

SPICE POWDER
Grind to a powder:
1 teaspoon cumin seeds
3 cloves
3 cardamom pods
2 (1-inch) cinnamon sticks

Still Waters

The boat jetty in Allepey was as we remembered it—the canals that led out to the back-waters still moss-green with algae, the floating carpet of water hyacinth, the small private motorboats nudging the larger passenger boats and mammoth rice barges. The air was thick with the smell of damp rot, spices, and wood smoke. In the tea shop nearby, a radio played what seemed to be the same sad song. It was as if nothing had changed.

The year was 1968 and the vast labyrinth of Kerala's backwaters was still largely unknown to the rest of the world. Visiting my mother's brother Vakkachan and his family in the heart of Kuttanad was, as always, the most thrilling part of our annual pilgrimage to Kerala from Bombay. My mother's family, Ettupara, is from Kuttanad, deep in the backwaters that had been mostly inaccessible until a couple of decades ago. Kuttanad was a waterlogged expanse of wetlands, reclaimed when the government constructed the embankments and serpentine waterways now connecting thousands of villages and far-flung paddy fields. Four rivers—the Pamba, Meenachil, Achankoil, and Manimala—flow into this region, and much of Kuttanad, situated about 5 feet below sea level, had been inundated with water for most of the year. The bunds promised the prosperity that the beleaguered farmers had hoped for. Kuttanad was now lush with verdant paddies and though many low-lying farms were still flooded during the monsoon, the farmers prospered.

My grandfather Kuriachan, a lawyer, had moved to Allepey with my grandmother, Mamikutty of Velliyara Parayil, where he started a practice in his house. Here, he held musical discourses with his lawyer friends and intellectuals and wrote and published a romantic novel. But Vakkachan, his second son, eventually moved back to the paddy fields and built a home for his expanding family, cultivating rice, tapioca, bananas, and other cash crops.

Vakkachan's home was where we were now headed. The trip had been planned days ahead by my mother's youngest brother, Thomachan. A small motorboat had been arranged to take us into R Block where the farm was situated. We were a large group, my grandmother, uncle, and the Allepey cousins, and it took us a while to settle into the boat. Finally, we began to move away from the pier with a noisy chug-chug and soon were out in the open waters.

At the junction, we turned into a narrow canal that led to R Block. Here, the waterways were hemmed in by land, and the coconut trees leaned inward, their fronds forming a canopy.

We were already in a waterworld where there were no roads or cars for miles around. Instead, little *valloms*, larger country boats, and rice barges were all we saw, each moving at their own pace. Our own boat began to slow down so we could observe the daily bustle of life in the backwaters.

Little thatched huts with neat, hedged yards and wooden piers spewed smoke from their chimneys; fishermen hauled up baskets of tiny, silvery fish; and high above us, a toddy tapper perched on a coconut tree, his feet bound with rope to help him ascend and descend. Tiny canoes darted across the water, and at the shores, women washed clothes while little children splashed about like water babies. My uncle told us that children in the backwaters learned to swim as they took their first steps.

As we progressed, the canal widened into a junction of waterways and we stopped at a little tea shop by the bank. The small thatched wooden shack had a glass-fronted cupboard in which snacks were kept on display. The only pieces of furniture were a long wooden bench and a few wooden stools set at a table. At the table sat a lone customer with his newspaper, occasionally reading out bits of information to no one in particular.

Tea shop in the back waters

We sat on the grass while the grown-ups found seats on the little stools. My grandmother stayed in the boat smoking the *beedi* she had cadged from the driver, studiously ignoring my mother's disapproving glares. The tea shop also served *kallu* and soon glasses of the sweet toddy were brought over, along with glasses of tea. I took my first sip of *kallu* and liked its sweet-and-sour fizz. A plate of *neyappams* arrived.

My uncle asked if there was anything else on the menu. The shopkeeper replied hesitantly that there was just the mashed tapioca and fish curry that the field laborers would come in for later. My uncle asked for some of this daily fare and the *meen vevichathu* simmering in a clay pot was served to us; it was cooked to perfection—sour, spicy, and smoky. We ate it with the *kappa* and with little loaves of sweet, country bread we dipped into the curry.

My uncle spoke of how R Block was built and my mother narrated the story of the men who had built these embankments, and what they had endured in those early years. Many years before, when large tracts of land were reclaimed for cultivation and habitation, stone bunds—much like the dikes in Holland—were built to protect the land. Occasionally, a few of the stones deep under the water would work loose, threatening to bring down an entire section of the bund. This meant that the surrounding fields would flood and destroy the crops the farming community had worked for the whole year.

It was then that a man would step up, strong and fearless, and offer to go down into the murky depths to put the dislodged stones back in place, thus saving the crops and the livelihood of the entire community. The man was usually a laborer of the paraya caste and, though his bravery would be recognized and his family rewarded, he rarely surfaced alive.

The tea shop's other customer looked up from his newspaper at this point and told us he knew of such a man, the great-uncle of his wife's sister's husband. Our eyes opened wide as he told us of the ceremony that preceded the man's descent into the waters. The villagers held an all-night vigil and the gods were invoked to protect the chosen man. Early next morning at an auspicious time, he made the descent, amidst the ululations and wails of the womenfolk.

Decades later, the complexities of this story would still haunt me. Had he really chosen to go into the still dark waters on this suicide mission? Had they flipped a coin to assign the chosen one? Did he have a family to mourn him? I also thought of the man with the newspaper. There had been anger and sadness on his face—but his voice had been curiously flat and without expression.

Later, we pulled away from the tea shop and branched off again and then again into smaller canals. The waterways narrowed as we traveled further and further into the interior. My mother pointed to a few traditional family homes—*tharavads* of families related to the Ettupara clan. The houses were large wooden structures with tiled roofs and long, open verandahs, and we could see framed photographs of saints and ancestors on the walls through the open windows as we passed by.

The narrow canals that connected these houses were bridged by coconut logs placed across their widths and I remembered the previous summer, trying to imitate my cousins who lived here as they ran across the logs in perfect motion.

Turning again into a narrow canal, where the water was a murky green, the boat slowed down at the wooden pier of my uncle's house.

Preparing Egg Roast/Mutta Roast (page 140)

POULTRY AND EGGS

Most rural homes in Kerala have a backyard, however tiny, with a few chickens or ducks scratching about. The country hens and ducks produce tasty eggs and meat. In cities, however, with frozen chicken parts available in supermarkets, many opt for their favorite cuts of mass-produced birds. While in the United States, I found it disappointing to cook with these large flavorless pieces of frozen chicken. I was happy when a friend introduced me to the Cornish hen which tastes remarkably like the small, Indian country fowl.

In Kerala, chicken and duck are cooked into curries with coconut milk or ground coconut and spices, sautéed with herbs and cashew nuts, or steam-roasted—the meat is seared with spices and oil, then allowed to cook in the steam of its own juices. Boneless and skinless cuts of chicken, or chicken with bone and skin on can be used for all the recipes according to preference.

Eggs of all types are relished by Syrian Christians—brown country hen eggs, duck eggs with curative properties, and tiny speckled quail eggs. A cousin once brought home a large pea-hen egg from his estate in Kerala which he said made a delicious omelet. Horrified, my children smuggled it away and made a nest for it in a shoebox, with visions of a pet peacock. A year later, the unhatched egg accidently fell and cracked open to reveal a powdery residue. We mourned the loss of the peacock that never was.

125

Kerala Chicken Curry

Kozhi Karri

This is a rich, creamy curry with a smooth blend of spices and coconut milk. Large cubes of potatoes can be added when the chicken is half cooked; they make a tasty accompaniment, as they absorb the flavors of the rich gravy. For a thicker gravy, reduce the water added to 2 cups. Serve with appams or Kerala parotta.

Heat the oil in a large pan, add the onions and fry for 1 minute, until soft and transparent.

Add the ginger and garlic pastes and fry for 1 minute. Add the spice paste and the spice powder and fry over low heat, stirring continuously, for 1 to 2 minutes, until the oil rises to the top.

Add the chicken and stir-fry for 3 to 5 minutes, until the pieces are coated with the spice mixture. Add the water, thin coconut milk, and salt. Simmer over low heat for 20 minutes, with the lid on.

When the chicken is tender, add the thick coconut milk and cook for a few more minutes.

Heat the coconut oil in a small skillet and add the mustard seeds. When they burst, add the shallots and curry leaves and fry until golden brown. Pour over the curry and stir in the lime juice.

Serves 4

¼ cup oil
2 onions, thinly sliced
1 tablespoon ginger paste
2 tablespoons garlic paste
1 (3-pound) chicken, cut into 12 pieces
4 cups water
4 cups thin coconut milk
1 tablespoon salt
1 cup thick coconut milk
1 tablespoon coconut oil
1 teaspoon mustard seeds
6 shallots, thinly sliced
6 curry leaves
1 tablespoon lime juice

SPICE PASTE

Grind to a smooth paste:
¼ cup ground coriander
1 teaspoon chilli powder
1 teaspoon ground turmeric
½ cup water

SPICE POWDER

Warm spices slightly in a small dry skillet and then grind to a powder:
2 (1-inch) cinnamon sticks
6 cloves
4 cardamom pods
1 teaspoon aniseed
1 teaspoon black peppercorns

Chicken Stew
Kozhi Ishtew

The ishtew, *influenced by the blander Western stew, has a subtle blend of whole spices and green chillis simmered in coconut milk. When entertaining, I like to use boneless chicken in bite-size pieces. Vegetable stew can also be prepared the same way with potatoes, carrots, cauliflower, and beans. Ishtew is usually served with appams or puttu, but is also good with thick slices of bread.*

Heat the oil in a deep pan and fry the sliced shallots until they are golden brown; remove them and set aside for garnishing.

In the same oil, fry the onion wedges for 1 to 2 minutes, until soft. Add the green chillis, ginger, and curry leaves and fry for 1 more minute. Add the cinnamon sticks, cardamom pods, and cloves and sauté for 1 minute, then add the flour and stir-fry for 1 minute.

Add the chicken pieces and stir-fry for 2 to 3 minutes until the meat is lightly seared. Add the potatoes, vinegar, water, thin coconut milk, and salt, and cook for 15 minutes over medium heat or until the chicken and potatoes are tender but firm.

Add the thick coconut milk and crushed peppercorns and simmer for 2 minutes.

Garnish with the fried shallots when serving.

NOTE: For a complete meal, add rice flour dumplings just before the thick coconut milk is added. To make the dumplings use the recipe for Steamed Rice Balls on page 39 and shape the mixture into bite-sized dumplings and lightly steam them before adding to the stew.

Serves 6

1 tablespoon oil
6 shallots, thinly sliced
2 onions, cut into thick wedges
3 green chillis, slit
1 tablespoon sliced fresh ginger
8 curry leaves
3 (1-inch) cinnamon sticks
4 cardamom pods, lightly crushed
6 whole cloves
½ tablespoon all-purpose flour
1 (3-pound) chicken, cut into 16 pieces or
    4 boneless chicken breasts, quartered
2 large potatoes, quartered
½ tablespoon vinegar
3 cups water
3 cups thin coconut milk
1 tablespoon salt
½ cup thick coconut milk
1 teaspoon crushed black peppercorns

Kerala Chicken Roast

Kozhi Roast

This traditional roast chicken is braised, fried with a host of spices, and then simmered in a thin gravy. Serve on a large platter with the mashed potatoes on the side, and garnish with fried onions. Thick slices of bread and an onion and tomato salad can accompany this dish.

Put the chicken pieces in a large pot with the water, coriander, chilli powder, turmeric, peppercorns, ginger, vinegar, and salt. Cook for 8 to 10 minutes over medium heat, or until the chicken is partially cooked and about 3 cups of liquid remains; remove from the heat.

Heat the oil in a large roasting pot, fry the onions and garlic for 2 to 3 minutes until golden brown. Remove the onions and garlic from the pan and set aside. In the same oil, lightly fry the tomatoes and then remove from the pan.

Remove the chicken pieces from their liquid and fry them in batches in the oil for 4 to 5 minutes, until lightly browned and crisp. Remove them from the oil as they cook and set aside.

When all the chicken has been fried, carefully pour the cooking liquid from the chicken into the oil and cook for 2 minutes. Add the fried chicken pieces, onions, garlic, and tomatoes and cook over low heat for 3 to 5 minutes, until the spicy gravy has browned and coated the chicken.

To make the mashed potatoes: In a bowl, mash the potatoes, then add the coconut milk, salt, and pepper. Mix until smooth.

Serves 4

1 (4-pound) roasting chicken, cut into 12 pieces
6 cups water
2 tablespoons ground coriander
1 teaspoon chilli powder
1 teaspoon ground turmeric
1 teaspoon crushed black peppercorns
1 teaspoon sliced fresh ginger
1 teaspoon vinegar
1 tablespoon salt
½ cup oil
2 large onions, sliced
6 cloves garlic, sliced
2 tomatoes, quartered and seeded

MASHED POTATOES:
4 large potatoes, boiled
1 cup thick coconut milk
½ teaspoon ground black pepper
½ teaspoon salt

Chicken Korma

Kozhi Kuruma

In this mildly spiced dish from the Malabar Muslim community, chicken is simmered in a blend of coconut, cashews, and poppy seeds. Serve with Kerala parotta *and a salad.*

Heat the oil in a deep cooking pot. Add the onions and fry for 2 to 3 minutes, until they are lightly browned.

Add the ginger and garlic pastes, tomatoes, and turmeric, and continue frying for 2 minutes. Add the coconut paste and fry for 2 minutes or until the oil rises to the top. Add the spice powder and stir-fry for 1 minute.

Add the chicken and salt and mix well until the chicken is well coated with the spice paste. Add the water and cook over a slow fire for 15 to 20 minutes, until the chicken is tender and the gravy is thick and creamy.

Serves 4

2 tablespoons oil
2 onions, finely chopped
1 tablespoon ginger paste
2 tablespoons garlic paste
2 tomatoes, chopped
1 teaspoon ground turmeric
1 (3-pound) chicken, cut into 12 pieces
1 tablespoon salt
6 cups water

COCONUT PASTE

Grind to a fine paste:
1 cup grated fresh coconut
½ cup chopped cashews
1 tablespoon poppy seeds
3 green chillis
¼ cup water

SPICE POWDER

Warm slightly in a small, dry skillet and then
    grind to a powder:
4 cloves
4 cardamom pods
1 small cinnamon stick
1 teaspoon aniseed

Chicken with Green Herbs

Thengayum Malli Ella Chertha Kozhi

The herb-and-coconut paste imparts a garden-fresh flavor and fragrance to this dish. Serve this chicken with rice and accompaniments.

Serves 4

Heat the oil in a large skillet. Add the onions and fry for 1 to 2 minutes, until they are soft.

Add the ginger and garlic and stir-fry for 2 to 3 minutes, until they are browned evenly. Add the coconut paste and fry for 2 minutes or until the oil rises to the top.

Add the chicken, salt, and spice powder. Mix well, cover, and cook for about 20 minutes over low heat, stirring occasionally, until the chicken is cooked and well seasoned.

Add the tomatoes, fry for another minute, and then remove from heat. Stir in the lime juice just before serving.

¼ cup oil
2 onions, sliced
1 teaspoon minced fresh ginger
2 teaspoons minced garlic
1 (2-pound) chicken, cut into 12 pieces
1 tablespoon salt
2 tomatoes, quartered and seeded
1 tablespoon lime juice

Coconut Paste

Grind to a fine paste with a little water:
½ cup grated coconut
1 cup fresh coriander leaves (cilantro)
¼ cup fresh mint leaves
4 green chillis

Spice Powder

Warm slightly in a small dry skillet and then grind to a powder:
6 cardamom pods
6 whole cloves
2 cinnamon sticks

Trivandrum Fried Chicken

A spicier version of an American favorite, Southern Fried Chicken, this dish is a restaurant favorite in Kerala. I got this recipe from a small wayside restaurant in Kochi, though the origins of this dish are unknown. I suppose some enterprising cook from Trivandrum, the capital city of Kerala, concocted this recipe and named it after his hometown.

Steaming the marinated chicken ensures that the meat inside is well cooked and also seals in the flavor. However, it is a step you can skip, instead marinating the meat for a few hours and then coating and frying as usual. Rice flour is used to coat the chicken as it makes the meat crisper than wheat flour. This chicken dish is perfect for picnics served with a salad.

Dry the chicken pieces with paper towels. Mix the marinade ingredients into a paste and rub all over the chicken pieces.

Bring water to a boil in the bottom of a steamer. Place the chicken pieces in the top of the steamer and steam the chicken for 5 to 8 minutes. (Alternatively, place the chicken to marinate in the refrigerator for a few hours before frying.)

Place the beaten egg mixture in one shallow bowl and the rice flour in another. Dip the chicken pieces into the beaten egg mixture and then coat with the rice flour.

When all the pieces are coated, heat the oil in a deep skillet and fry the chicken in batches for 3 to 5 minutes over medium heat, until crisp and golden.

Serves 4

6 whole chicken legs (leg and thigh),
    halved at the joint
1 egg beaten with ¼ cup water
1 cup rice flour
Oil for deep-frying

MARINADE:
1 tablespoon ground coriander
1 teaspoon chilli powder
1 teaspoon ground turmeric
1 teaspoon garlic paste
1 tablespoon lime juice
1 teaspoon salt

Pepper Chicken Roast

Kurumolagu Chertha Kozhi Roast

The Kerala roasting technique—using a heavy, lidded skillet—is used here to cook the chicken with a few select spices and its own steam to seal in the juices. This dish is especially good with the chicken skin left on to slowly crisp and brown. It is essential to fry the onions until they are evenly browned to make the dish a true success. Serve as a main dish with fried julienned potatoes, rice, and accompaniments.

In a large skillet, fry the onions in the oil for 2 to 3 minutes, until they are lightly browned.

Add the whole garlic and continue frying for 2 more minutes, until the onions and garlic are dark brown.

Add the red chillis, sauté lightly, then add the chicken, salt, peppercorns, and cinnamon sticks. Mix well and cook covered over low heat for 20 minutes, lifting the lid every 5 minutes to stir and toss, until the chicken pieces are tender and coated with the browned onion and pepper mix.

Serves 4 to 6

½ cup oil
8 onions, sliced
6 cloves garlic
8 red chillis, halved
6 whole chicken legs (legs and thighs), halved at the joint
1 teaspoon salt
1 tablespoon cracked black peppercorns
2 (1-inch) cinnamon sticks

Chicken Cooked in Toasted Coconut Gravy

Varatharache Kozhi Karri

This is a rich flavorful chicken curry from the Malabar region that is made for special occasions. The chicken simmers in a roasted coconut and spice mix that gives the dish its complex flavors. Serve as a main dish with pathiri, rice or appams.

Season the chicken pieces with the turmeric and salt. Set aside to marinate for 1 hour.

PREPARE THE COCONUT PASTE:

Roast the coconut in a heavy pan, stirring continously till it turns golden brown. Remove and set aside to cool. Heat 1 tablespoon of the coconut oil in the same pan, add the onions and cook till translucent. Add the garlic and ginger and cook for 2 minutes more. Add the tomatoes and green chillies and stir till it cooks into a soft mass. Take off the heat.

Grind the roasted coconut with a little water till it is smooth. Add the tomato mixture till it all blends together. Heat the rest of the coconut oil, add the roasted coconut mixture and cook for 2 minutes. Add the coriander powder, chilli powder, and ground fennel seeds, and stir well as it cooks until the oil separates.

PREPARE THE CHICKEN:

Add the chicken to the coconut paste and add the salt and cook for 3 minutes till the chicken pieces are coated with the paste. Add the water and cook for 15 minutes or until the meat is tender.

Add the spice powder to the chicken. Cover and cook for an additional 5 minutes.

PREPARE SEASONINGS:

Heat the 1 teaspoon coconut oil in a small pan. Add the mustard seeds and when they burst add the shallots and curry leaves. Cook for 1 minute and pour over the chicken. Serve.

Serves 4

1 (about 2.5-pound) chicken, cut into 12 pieces
1 teaspoon turmeric powder
1 tablespoon salt
1 teaspoon salt
3 cups water

COCONUT PASTE
½ cup grated coconut
¼ cup coconut oil
1 large onion, chopped
1 tablespoon garlic, coarsely ground
1 tablespoon ginger, coarsely ground
2 tomatoes, chopped
2 green chillies, chopped
2 tablespoons coriander powder
½ teaspoon chilli powder
1 teaspoon fennel seeds, ground

SPICE POWDER
Toast spices over low heat for 1 minute and then grind.
4 cloves
1 cinnamon stick
4 cardamom pods
1 teaspoon black peppercorns

SEASONINGS
1 teaspoon coconut oil
½ teaspoon mustard seeds
4 shallots, sliced
12 curry leaves

Chicken with Thick Gravy

Kozhi Peralen

This is a classic country-style chicken dish with a thick gravy, a method of cooking called a peralen. *Serve with rice and accompaniments.*

Mix the spice paste with the chicken, shallots, ginger, garlic, vinegar, and salt in a medium wide pot. Add the water and simmer over medium heat for 8 minutes or until the water has reduced to about 2 cups. Remove the chicken from the pan and reserve the gravy.

Heat the oil in a small skillet and add the mustard seeds. When they burst, add the sliced onion and curry leaves and fry for 1 to 2 minutes, until lightly browned.

Add the chicken pieces without the gravy and fry for 5 minutes or until the meat is lightly browned. Add the gravy and cook for 2 more minutes, until the curry is thick and creamy.

Serves 4 to 6

1 (3-pound) chicken, cut into 15 pieces
½ cup sliced shallots
½ teaspoon sliced fresh ginger
8 cloves garlic, sliced
1 teaspoon vinegar
1 tablespoon salt
6 cups water
¼ cup coconut oil
2 teaspoons mustard seeds
1 large onion, sliced
12 curry leaves

SPICE PASTE

Warm spices slightly in a small, dry skillet and then grind with the water to a smooth paste:
2 tablespoons ground coriander
1 teaspoon chilli powder
½ teaspoon ground turmeric
½ teaspoon finely ground black pepper
¼ teaspoon cumin seeds
1 small cinnamon stick
4 cardamom pods
6 cloves
¼ teaspoon aniseed
¼ cup water

Cashew Chicken

Kashu Andi Chertha Kozhi

This mildly spiced chicken dish is made with pureed cashews. The recipe was given to me by a friend from Quilon, the cashew capital of Kerala. Much of the country's cashews are grown in this region and their creamy whiteness in this dish forms the perfect backdrop for the bright colors of the seasoning, making this a spectacular dish for entertaining. Serve with parotta or pathiri and a salad, though the dish is delicious any way you serve it. I have even spooned it over pasta, seasoning included!

Sprinkle the chicken pieces with the salt. Heat 2 tablespoons of the oil in a heavy skillet and stir-fry the chicken pieces over high heat for 3 to 5 minutes, until the meat is seared—do not brown.

Lower the heat and add the cashew paste. Stir-fry to combine and gradually add the yogurt. Continue frying for 2 to 3 minutes, until the oil rises to the top.

Stir in the spice powder and continue cooking with the lid on for 5 to 8 minutes, until the chicken is tender, lifting the lid occasionally to stir and sprinkle in some water. Pour into a serving dish.

Heat 1 teaspoon of the oil in a small skillet and add the mustard seeds. When they burst, add the halved cashews and fry until they are golden brown. Add the curry leaves and red chillis and remove from the heat immediately. Pour over the cooked chicken but do not stir.

NOTE: Do not allow any of the principal ingredients— yogurt, cashews, chicken—to brown as this will add color to the creamy whiteness of this dish.

Serves 4

8 boneless chicken breasts, cut into 1-inch cubes
1 teaspoon salt
2 tablespoons oil plus 1 teaspoon
1 cup plain yogurt
½ cup water
1 teaspoon oil
½ teaspoon mustard seeds
6 unroasted cashew halves
6 curry leaves
2 red chillis, torn in half

CASHEW PASTE

Puree into a paste:
2 cup unroasted cashews, soaked for 2 hours and drained
2 onions, chopped
2 green chillis
8 cloves garlic
1 small piece fresh ginger
½ cup water

SPICE POWDER

Warm slightly in a small, dry skillet and then grind to a powder:
2 cardamom pods
4 whole cloves
1 (1-inch) cinnamon stick

Fried Quail
Kaada Varathathu

Many poultry shops in smaller towns in Kerala sell quail, partridge, and other game birds. This recipe can be used for any small bird, including Cornish hen. Serve with *parotta and a salad.*

Make a paste of the chilli powder, ground pepper, salt, and vinegar. Rub this mixture all over the quails and set aside for 1 hour.

Bring water to a boil in the bottom of a steamer. Place the quails in the top of the steamer and steam the birds for 5 minutes, until the flesh is firm.

Heat the oil in a large skillet. Add the quails, cover, and fry over low heat for 5 to 8 minutes on each side, until the birds turn a dark golden brown.

Serves 2

1 tablespoon chilli powder
1 teaspoon ground black pepper
1 teaspoon salt
1 tablespoon vinegar
2 quails, about 1 pound each
1 cup oil

Duck Roast
Tharavu Roast

Duck is usually served at festive occasions in Kerala—a wedding lunch, Christmas, or Easter. Though duck is commercially raised and available at supermarkets in Kerala, many homes in rural areas have a few ducks along with chickens and a turkey in the backyard, where they are fed with scraps of food from the kitchen. The tastiest ducks reportedly come from Kumarakom, in the backwaters near Kottayam, where hunters go for a day of duckshooting. My cousin Thommachen shot off one of his fingers on a hunt here, in his early hunting days—which made him a hero in our eyes when he visited us in Bombay!

This recipe uses a spiced water infusion, in which the duck is simmered and then fried. My cousin Binny made this traditional Duck Roast when we prepared the photo shoot for this book, and later we sat down to lunch. Yes, it was as succulent and delicious as the picture promises. Serve with sliced fried potatoes on the side.

Put the duck in a heavy-bottomed wide pot with the spice powder and all the other ingredients except the oil and onions. Partially cover and cook for 20 to 30 minutes over low heat.

When the duck is tender and the gravy has been reduced to 2 cups, remove from the heat. Remove the duck from the pan and reserve the gravy.

Heat the oil in a large skillet and fry the sliced onions for 3 to 4 minutes, until golden brown; remove them and set aside.

In the same oil, fry the duck pieces in batches for 4 to 5 minutes, until they brown. Remove the duck pieces and set aside.

When all the duck has been fried, pour the gravy into the oil and cook for 2 minutes or until it has thickened. Add the duck and the fried onions, stir and cook for 5 minutes, until the meat is coated with the gravy.

Serves 6

1 (4-pound) duck, cut into 12 to 15 pieces
3 tablespoons sliced fresh ginger
12 cloves garlic, sliced
6 green chillis, chopped
12 curry leaves
3 tablespoons vinegar
2 tablespoons crushed black peppercorns
2 tablespoons salt
12 cups water
½ cup oil
4 large onions, sliced

SPICE POWDER

Warm slightly in a small, dry skillet and then grind to a powder:
6 cardamom pods
5 whole cloves
2 (1-inch) cinnamon sticks

Kerala Turkey Roast

Kalkam Roast

In Kerala, turkey is jointed and cooked into a curry, or roasted in a large urali with a liberal dose of spices, much like roast chicken or duck. When Sara, a Syrian Christian friend from California, gave me this recipe, I was intrigued by her combining of Western cooking practices with Indian herbs and spices. In true pioneering spirit, she had adapted the original recipe to create this dish for a Thanksgiving meal at her home, with a twist to the traditional accompaniments—a pilau-like rice stuffing fragrant with spices and fresh coriander leaves. Serve the turkey with roasted potatoes, rice stuffing, and gravy.

BEGIN BRINING 2 DAYS AHEAD:

Using enough water to cover the top of the turkey, mix the brining ingredients in a very large pot and bring to a boil. Simmer and stir for 5 minutes and then remove from the heat and cool completely. Add the turkey to the pot, cover, and refrigerate overnight.

The next day, remove the turkey from the brine and place on a rack in a roasting pan. Cover and refrigerate again overnight.

Preheat the oven to 350 degrees F.

MAKE THE MARINADE:

Heat the butter in a small pan, remove from the heat, and whisk in the remaining marinade ingredients until smooth and glossy.

Brush this marinade on the turkey. Remove the rack from the roasting pan and place the turkey directly in the roasting pan with the wings tucked under and the legs tied together loosely. Roast for 1 hour, then brush more marinade liberally over the turkey. Roast for another hour until it begins to brown. Brush on additional

Serves 12

1 (20-pound) turkey with skin
Potatoes (desired amount), cut in half

BRINE:
Enough water to cover the turkey
8 bay leaves
12 cloves
24 whole peppercorns
6 red chillis, halved
2 cups apple cider
1 cup salt

MARINADE:
1 cup butter
3 tablespoons chilli powder
1 tablespoon crushed black peppercorns
¼ cup prepared mustard
¼ cup garlic paste
¼ cup dark brown sugar
3 tablespoons salt

STUFFING:
1½ pounds half-cooked long-grain rice
1 cup thick coconut milk
1 cup chopped onion
1 cup toasted chopped nuts (cashews, peanuts, almonds)
3 cinnamon sticks
½ cup chopped coriander leaves (cilantro)

marinade and cover with foil. Roast until an instant-read thermometer inserted into the thickest part of the thigh registers 175 degrees F.

MEANWHILE, MAKE THE STUFFING:

In a large bowl, combine all the stuffing ingredients.

Once the turkey registers 175 degrees F, stuff the cavity of the turkey with the stuffing. Stitch the opening together, cover with foil, and continue roasting the turkey for 3 more hours, brushing with the marinade every 30 minutes and adding some water to the pan if the drippings begin to burn. Be sure to replace the foil covering after each addition.

Place the potato halves along the sides of the turkey 1 hour before the end of the cooking time.

Remove the roasting pan from the oven and let the turkey stand covered with foil for 1 hour. Remove the turkey and potatoes from the pan and transfer to a platter.

MAKE THE GRAVY:

Stir the chopped onions, flour, chicken broth, and cream into the roasting pan to combine with the drippings. Add salt if needed, and cook until slightly thickened. Blend the gravy in a food processor until smooth.

GRAVY:
1 cup finely chopped onion
¼ cup all-purpose flour
3 cups chicken broth
1 cup cream

Egg Roast
Mutta Roast

Perfectly browned onions are the base of this slowly stir-fried egg dish. This is a favorite in little tea shops and truck driver's haunts all over Kerala, usually served with parotta *or* appams. *Bakeries sometimes stuff the spiced eggs into triangles of flaky pastry and sell them as egg puffs, which are just as delicious.* Serve with *puttu, appams, and* parotta.

Heat the oil in a skillet and add the onions. Stirring continuously, sauté the onions over medium heat for 3 to 5 minutes or until they are lightly browned.*

Add the garlic, ginger, tomatoes, and curry leaves, and continue frying for 2 minutes or until the onions are a darker brown.

Mix the chilli powder, turmeric, fennel, peppercorns, and salt in a small bowl, adding just enough water to make a thick paste. Add this to the onion mixture along with the shelled eggs.

Continue frying for 1 to 2 minutes, until the onions and spices have blended and coated the eggs. Halve the eggs and serve.

Serves 4

¼ cup oil
3 cups thinly sliced onions
4 cloves garlic, sliced
½ teaspoon slivered fresh ginger
2 tomatoes, quartered and seeded
12 curry leaves
1 teaspoon chilli powder
½ teaspoon ground turmeric
1 teaspoon ground fennel seeds
½ teaspoon coarsely crushed black peppercorns
1 teaspoon salt
6 hard-boiled eggs, shelled

*TIP FOR BROWNING ONIONS EVENLY:
Stir the onions continuously over medium to high heat, adding a few spoonfuls of water as they brown; this prevents the onions from burning and adds moisture. It also speeds up the process, though this may also depend on the heat and the vessel used. I use a heavy steel pan and alternate between medium to high heat.

Country Omelet
Naaden Omlet

Rustle this up for a quick snack or when an extra dish is needed. The coconut oil, shallots, and curry leaves are what make this simple dish truly special.

Kandhari, the small fiery chillis from Kerala, can be added instead of regular green chillis, if available. The eggs (chicken or duck) can be made in one thick single omelet, divided into smaller omelets, or even scrambled. This spicy omelet is delicious with crusty bread, puttu, warm parottas, or as a side dish with rice and accompaniments.

Serves 2 to 3

2 tablespoons coconut oil
½ cup sliced shallots
1 teaspoon chopped green chillis
8 curry leaves, torn
5 eggs, beaten
½ teaspoon salt
½ teaspoon crushed black peppercorns

Heat the oil in a large skillet. Add the shallots and fry for 1 minute.

Add the green chillis and curry leaves, and continue to fry over low heat for a few more minutes.

Mix the beaten eggs with the salt and pepper. Turn up the heat and add the eggs to the skillet. Cook the eggs until beginning to set, lifting the sides of the omelet with a spatula to let the eggs run underneath the cooked portions. Flip the omelet over and cook the other side briefly.

Fold the omelet in half and cut into thick wedges. Serve hot.

VARIATIONS: Though a simple country-style omelet is delicious by itself, it can be elevated with the addition of these ingredients: sliced and caramelized shallots; chopped mushrooms, spinach, or tomatoes lightly sautéed in coconut oil; or leftover sautéed minced beef or prawns. Add these when the omelet is still runny, and cover with a lid till done.

Ritual Baths

Syrian Christians have long celebrated the arrival of a newborn with time-honored traditions and rituals. Though many of these traditions have been lost, the ritual baths and massages which nurture and revitalize the new mother have prevailed—and for good reason. The forty days after childbirth spent in the new mother's parent's home is a time of joy and bonding, a time for special foods, rigorous massages, and languid baths.

For many weeks, the house prepares for the arrival of the mother and child. The *kulapir chedathi* (the bathing woman) arrives, oils and powders are readied, and the bedroom and bathing room of the new mother is made ready. Most young mothers love the pampering and indulge in the sheer luxury of being cared for. In your mother's house, there are many hands to help, and during this short time you are allowed to forget the responsibility of caring for the new baby. The *chedathi*, long experienced in matters of childbirth and familiar with the ways of your family, takes over and you are in her capable hands.

Special baths start as soon as the child is born, or in modern times, when the mother and child are brought home from the hospital. The process begins around ten in the morning when the sun has risen high. The *dhanvanthari thailam*, a medicated oil prepared especially for this purpose, is warmed and lavishly applied all over the new mother's body, followed by a vigorous massage which lasts for an hour. Every muscle and tired bone is kneaded and coaxed to life under strong, supple hands, leaving the skin polished and glistening with the luminous red oil. No corner is left unmassaged— the temples, the neck, the bump behind the ears, the small of the back, down to the toes. The head is then massaged with herbal coconut oil and finally with a flourish, the hair is tied into a topknot.

Ammini, who massaged and bathed me and my three daughters, was built like a wrestler, with large, supple hands and smooth, dark skin that glistened from the oils of a thousand massages. At her mercy, I sat on the wooden stool in the bathing room while she recounted her travel stories which ranged from rustic country homes in the backwaters of Kuttanad to opulent villas in distant Dubai. Pulling away the oily magazine I would sneak in, she would admonish me. "No reading at this time! The brain is weak after childbirth and likely to absorb the wrong matter." Ammini preferred to keep me entertained herself, discussing everything from food preparations to politics.

After the massage, while the mother's skin absorbs the rich oil, the baby is placed on a bathing mat and massaged with a lighter oil. Babies enjoy this gentle touch and are relaxed and placid throughout the massage. The oil is removed with a paste of chickpea flour, then the baby is briskly toweled and delivered to waiting hands.

The mother is washed down with *inja*—a soapy, fibrous loofah—or chickpea paste which is milder than soap and hot, herb-infused water. *Shikakai* (soap plant) is used to wash the hair clean of its oils, though much of it stays on for weeks and even months. Washed and scrubbed clean, the mother steps into the bedroom where frankincense resin is placed on embers, the resulting fragrance purifying the air.

A rich, nourishing broth of chicken or mutton is given to the mother. This varies in each house. In my grandmother's house in Kanjirapally, mutton was put in a large *barani* (ceramic jar) with cinnamon, cloves, ginger, garlic, and pepper. This was placed in a large cauldron of water and simmered on the back stove of the hearth for days, until the meat fell off its bones. She made this rich broth for her own daughters who had many babies and sometimes even for her son's wives who were no less prolific. Considering I have eighty-three cousins on my father's side, the children of her eleven sons and daughters, that hearth must certainly have been kept busy!

After each birth, Ammini ruled the house with an iron fist. Entrusted with the important task of caring for the mother and child, she demanded that meals be on time, loud voices be subdued, and guests who overstayed be shooed off. Nothing was allowed to hamper the well-being of her two wards. Visiting husbands were not encouraged to stay with the new mother in her room and a less determined husband than mine would have given up. Standing guard outside my room in case I needed her while he was there, Ammini wore an air of resigned disapproval, her arms crossed over her ample bosom and a frown on her face.

Late at night, when handing the baby over for nursing, she would talk of her idealistic but perpetually out-of-work husband, her handicapped son, and her one hope—the bright young daughter she prayed would one day get them all out of the rut.

A strong bond was forged between us, formed during long baths and late night nursings. After each confinement, when the forty days were past and I was well enough to leave, I would plead with Ammini to accompany me to my own home. "I don't know how to bathe the new baby all by myself," I would moan. "And I can't take care of the baby and her sisters who are still babies themselves." But Ammini would shake her head. She had another birth to attend to, another young mother and child waiting for her strong, caring hands.

Parottas (page 154) cooking on a large restaurant griddle

ACCOMPANIMENTS

Eaten with the staples of rice, meat, and vegetables, accompaniments make a piquant addition to every meal—spiced buttermilk to be mixed with rice, crisp pappadams, vinegary onion salad, fresh fruit jams for breakfast and tea, and tangy crushed or ground chutneys prepared with coconut, green mangoes, tomatoes, or shallots.

Chamandhis (chutneys) are freshly prepared for a meal or stored away in bottles along with pickles. Bitter gourd, eggplant, and green banana can be crisply fried and kept for up to a month. Plain or cooked buttermilk can also be kept refrigerated for days. *Pappadams* are fried or roasted to be served immediately. Soup is usually a rich broth made with mutton or chicken, simmered with spices with a light seasoning of fried shallots. Black coffee sweetened with molasses and sweet milky tea are brewed fresh, though a little *kalam* (pot) of black coffee may be kept aside for the unexpected visitor.

Tropical fruits like papayas, mangoes, pineapples, and guavas, which grow in abundance through the year, are puréed and simmered into jellies and jams, or made into fruit squashes to be diluted with iced water for guests.

Soft, flaky Kerala *parottas* are one of the few wheat breads in a predominantly rice-based diet, hence they have been included in this chapter as an accompaniment to curries and fried dishes.

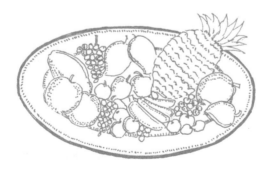

Buttermilk
Moru

Lightly spiced buttermilk—beaten yogurt diluted with water—is a refreshing drink and the ideal accompaniment for a spicy meal. Serve with a meal, or as a cool summer drink diluted even further with a cup of water or ice.

In a medium bowl, beat the yogurt with the water and salt. Using a mortar and pestle, coarsely crush the green chillis, curry leaves, and ginger. Add this mixture to the yogurt mixture and chill for an hour before serving.

Serves 2 to 3

2 cups plain yogurt
1 cup water
½ teaspoon salt
2 green chillis, chopped
6 curry leaves
1 teaspoon minced fresh ginger

Spiced Cooked Buttermilk
Moru Kachiyathu

A pitcher of this lightly cooked buttermilk is a must at any Syrian Christian meal. This can also be made without coconut, following the same recipe. Serve with rice, vegetable thorans, *and fried fish or meat.*

In a deep saucepan, mix the yogurt with the water and salt. Add the coconut paste, mix well, and cook over low heat, stirring continuously, for 2 minutes or until it is just warmed. Remove from the heat immediately.

Heat the oil in a small skillet and add the mustard seeds. When they burst, add the fenugreek seeds and shallots and brown lightly. Add the curry leaves and red chillis and when the chillis turn bright red, pour this mixture into the warmed yogurt. Pour into a pitcher to serve.

Serves 4

4 cups plain yogurt, beaten
1 cup water
½ teaspoon salt
1 teaspoon oil
1 teaspoon mustard seeds
½ teaspoon fenugreek seeds
1 tablespoon sliced shallots
6 curry leaves
2 red chillis, torn into large pieces

COCONUT PASTE

Grind to a fine paste with a little water:
¼ cup grated fresh coconut
3 green chillis
1 teaspoon chopped fresh ginger
½ teaspoon ground turmeric
¼ teaspoon cumin seeds

Spiced Yogurt
Molagu Thairu

Thick, undiluted yogurt (called Greek yogurt in the U.S.) should be used for this spicy accompaniment from Palghat district on the Kerala border. I often use this recipe with hung curd or soft cottage cheese to make a spicy dip. Serve with rice, vegetable thorans, and pappadam.

Serves 4

4 cups thick (Greek) plain yogurt
½ teaspoon salt
2 tablespoons oil
4 cloves garlic, chopped
4 red chillis, broken into pieces
4 curry leaves
¼ teaspoon asafoetida

Mix the yogurt and salt in a bowl.

Heat the oil in a small skillet. Add the garlic and fry for 1 minute. When it browns, add the red chillis and curry leaves. When the chillis turn a deep red (in about 5 seconds) add the asafoetida and immediately remove from the heat.

Blend this mixture with a mortar and pestle or in a food processor until it is coarsely crushed. Pour it into the yogurt and lightly stir in.

Dried Shrimp Chutney
Onakka Chemmeen Chamandhi

Dried shrimps have an intense flavor that is enhanced by coarsely ground coconut. The chutney should be dry and crumbly, the ingredients just lightly crushed. Serve fresh, as this chutney does not keep for long. Serve at meals as a fresh accompaniment.

Makes 1½ cups

1 cup dried shrimps
1 cup grated fresh coconut
3 green chillis
6 shallots, sliced

In a small skillet, lightly toast the dried shrimps over low heat for 2 minutes. Blend all the ingredients together in a spice grinder until the mixture is coarse and crumbly. Taste and add salt only if needed, as the dried shrimps will be salty.

Tomato Chutney
Thakali Chamandhi

This freshly prepared chutney has a surprise ingredient—sesame seeds, which adds a nutty, creamy texture when puréed. Serve as an accompaniment at a meal; tomato chutney is also delicious as a sandwich filler or dip.

Heat the oil in a pan. Add the onion and fry for 1 minute or until transparent.

Add the garlic, fry for 1 minute, then add the chilli powder, turmeric, and asafoetida and fry over low heat until the oil rises to the top.

Add the chopped tomatoes and salt and cook for 2 to 3 minutes. Remove from the heat and set aside to cool.

Once the tomato mixture is cool, add the toasted sesame seeds and purée in a blender until thick and smooth.

Garnish with the chopped coriander before serving.

Makes 4 cups

2 tablespoons oil
1 onion, chopped
6 cloves garlic
1 tablespoon chilli powder
½ teaspoon ground turmeric
½ teaspoon asafoetida
6 cups coarsely chopped tomatoes
1 teaspoon salt
½ cup toasted sesame seeds
½ cup chopped fresh coriander (cilantro), to garnish

Green Mango Chutney
Pacha Manga Chamandhi

Sour green mangoes and even salted green mangoes can be used for this tangy chutney. If salted mangoes are used, do not add salt. This chutney is usually freshly prepared and served with Kerala Biryani.

Blend all the ingredients in a food processor until smooth and creamy.

Makes ¾ cup

½ cup grated fresh coconut
1 cup peeled and chopped green mango
1 teaspoon chopped fresh ginger
3 green chillis, chopped
¼ cup water
1 teaspoon salt

Date and Raisin Chutney

Eenthapazhamum Munthiringa Chamandhi

This sweet and spicy chutney from the Cannanore region can be kept for up to a week in the refrigerator. Serve with fish or mutton biryani or as a dip.

In a small bowl, soak the dates and raisins in the vinegar for 2 hours.

Heat the oil in a small pan. Add the garlic and ginger and fry for 1 minute. Add the chilli powder and salt and immediately remove from heat.

Blend all the ingredients together in a food processor until smooth or chunky, according to your preference.

Set aside for 2 hours before serving.

Makes 1 cup

1 cup chopped dates
½ cup raisins
¼ cup vinegar
1 teaspoon oil
6 cloves garlic, chopped
1 teaspoon chopped fresh ginger
1 tablespoon chilli powder
1 teaspoon salt

Shallot Chutney

Ulli Chamandhi

This coarsely crushed fresh chutney is best prepared with a mortar and pestle. Coconut oil enhances the flavor of the ingredients, but any other oil can be used. Fiery kandhari chillis can be used for a spicier chutney. Serve with boiled tapioca or sweet potato.

Crush the shallots and green chillis in a mortar, gradually adding the other ingredients. Place the crushed mixture in a serving bowl and add the slightly warmed oil. Stir to mix.

The chutney should be kept for an hour to mellow before serving.

Makes ¾ cup

1 cup halved shallots
8 green chillis, torn into pieces
½ cup vinegar
1 teaspoon sea salt
2 teaspoons coconut oil, slightly warmed

Coconut and Curry Leaf Chutney Powder

Vepilakatti

This dry chutney powder can be kept for months in an air-tight container. The coconut should be evenly roasted until golden brown and the moisture has evaporated. When I was away at college, I took jars of this spicy, sweet-and-sour chutney powder to spice up dreary meals. My friends had a nickname for the fiery dark brown chutney—gunpowder! Serve as an accompaniment with any rice-based meal.

Dry-roast the coconut in a heavy-bottomed large skillet over medium heat for 5 to 8 minutes, stirring continuously so the coconut is evenly browned.

When the coconut turns a golden brown, add the curry leaves and red chillis. Continue stirring, scooping up the mixture from the bottom to avoid burning. When the mixture is evenly browned, add the rest of the ingredients and stir well. Remove from the heat and set aside to cool. Once cool, place mixture in a food processor and process for 1 minute and then spread out on a tray to dry.

When the mixture has dried, stir well to remove lumps. The chutney powder should resemble coarse dark brown bread crumbs. Store the powder in clean, dry bottles with tight-fitting lids.

Makes 6 cups

6 cups grated fresh coconut
3 cups curry leaves
12 whole red chillis
¼ cup whole black peppercorns
½ cup tamarind paste
3 tablespoons sugar
2 tablespoons salt

Jar Soup

Barani Soup

Kerala does not have a tradition of preparing soups so this is a rare exception. This is the nourishing broth my grandmother made for her daughters during the forty days after childbirth, to be had after the traditional oil bath (see pages 142–143). Traditionally simmered in a barani *(ceramic jar) which is sealed shut with a paste of dough, the soup can also be cooked in a large stockpot. After the broth has been strained, the mutton bones with soft meat and chopped liver can be stir-fried with onions and a spoon of crushed black peppercorns and eaten separately. My mother made this soup for her own daughters with tiny chickens, which made for a lighter broth.*

But no, you do not have to go through childbirth or the forty days of oil baths to savor this delicious soup! This is a nourishing broth to be served any time of the year, for any occasion.

Put all the ingredients in a large stockpot, cover and simmer over low heat for 3 hours.

Remove from heat and strain the soup, discarding the solids before serving the broth.

Serves 4

1 pound mutton bones with meat
¼ pound liver, chopped
3 onions, chopped
2 whole bay leaves
1 tablespoon chopped fresh ginger
12 cloves garlic, chopped
2 cinnamon sticks
6 cloves
1 tablespoon crushed black peppercorns
1½ teaspoons salt
12 cups water

Fried Bitter Gourd

Pavakka Varathathu

Bitter gourd is one of the favorite vegetables of Malayalis, and this is one method of storing them—as crisp fried rounds, ready to be eaten.

Bitter gourd has to be steamed lightly to remove some of its bitterness. The coconut slices are optional and are best if tender. In Kerala, coconut oil is used to deep-fry this delectable accompaniment, but any other oil can be substituted. The method used here also works for frying other produce such as julienned eggplant, raw banana slices, and sliced kovakka (ivy gourd); however, these vegetables do not need to be steamed first.

Fried bitter gourd can be served hot at a meal or be kept for weeks, stored in clean dry bottles.

Bring some water to a boil in the bottom of a steamer. Mix all the ingredients except the oil in the basket of a steamer and steam for 2 minutes.

Heat the oil in a deep pot. Add the bitter gourd mixture in batches and fry for 3 to 4 minutes, until golden brown. Drain on paper towels.

Serves 4

6 large bitter gourds, thinly sliced, pith removed
½ cup sliced coconut
6 shallots, sliced
3 green chillis
12 curry leaves
1 teaspoon ground turmeric
1 teaspoon salt
Oil for deep-frying

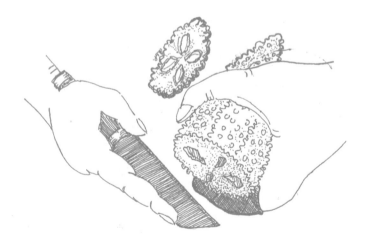

Onion Salad
Challas

Traditonal Kerala cuisine has no salads to boast of; this simple onion salad is perhaps the only exception. Finely shredded cabbage or thin wedges of tomato can be added as a variation. This onion salad can also be prepared with a dressing of watery yogurt instead of vinegar and coconut oil. That version is usually served with biryani. Challas *perfectly complements crisp fried fish and meats.*

Soak the onions in a cup of water for 10 minutes to reduce some of their pungency. Squeeze out the water and mix the onions with the other ingredients. Set aside for an hour before serving.

VARIATION: For a yogurt dressing, add 1 cup of watery yogurt instead of the vinegar and coconut oil.

Serves 4

2 large onions, sliced very thin
3 green chillis, seeded and cut in thin slivers
2 tablespoons vinegar
½ tablespoon coconut oil (*optional*)
½ teaspoon salt

Flaky Kerala Flatbread
Parotta

Wheat is rarely used in Kerala cuisine, but this delightfully flaky bread (perhaps of Middle Eastern origin) is an exception. The dough is folded, stretched, coiled, and then rolled into thick disks and cooked on a griddle. The flatbreads are then crushed lightly to fluff them up, which makes them soft and flaky.

This is popular restaurant and teashop fare that is delicious plain or with any dish—from a spicy omelet to a chicken or mutton curry. Kothu parotta, chopped parotta, is a popular street food that is served in handcarts near busy junctions in Kerala. The parotta is torn into small pieces and sautéed in a large griddle with onions, green chillis, and shredded curried meat, and an egg is thrown in for good measure. The result is a mess of deliciously crisp morsels.

Though I sometimes order fresh parottas from the local Kerala restaurant and freeze any extras for later, after preparing them at home on one occasion, I was rather pleased with the result. Also try this recipe with whole-wheat flour. Serve with any curry or fried dish.

Makes 8 to 10

4 cups all-purpose flour
½ teaspoon salt
½ teaspoon baking powder
1 teaspoon sugar
1 egg, beaten
1 cup oil
1 cup water, plus more as needed

In a large bowl, sift the flour twice with the salt and baking powder.

Mix in the sugar, egg, ¼ cup of the oil, and enough water to make a soft, pliable dough. Cover the dough with a damp cloth and set aside for an hour.

Shape the dough into 2-inch balls and coat them with oil. Cover with a damp cloth for another hour.

On an oiled surface, stretch each ball of dough into a long flat rope. Fold and stretch the dough, adding a little oil as you roll it into a ball again. Shape each ball into a thick rope once more, stretch and coil it around itself, like a flat turban. After all the coils are prepared, roll them out into ½-inch-thick disks.

Cook the flatbreads on a hot griddle for 1 to 2 minutes, until lightly browned on both sides. Remove from the griddle and crush in a dish towel. Serve hot.

Banana Jelly

Pazham Jam

Banana jelly is made with small palayamkodan *bananas which are often available at Kerala grocery stores. The jelly has a thick, syrupy consistency and turns a deep coffee color when ready. Serve with* puttu *or* idiappams, *or spread on thick slices of bread.*

Put the bananas and water in a deep pan and cook for 5 minutes over medium heat.

Remove from the heat and strain through a fine muslin cloth. (NOTE: Do not press to extract the liquid, as it will cloud the jelly—instead let the juice slowly drip into a bowl overnight. The resulting liquid should amount to 4 cups.)

Put the banana juice in a deep pan. Add the sugar and lemon juice and stir and cook over medium heat until it registers 215 degrees F when tested with a candy thermometer. The jelly should now be dark brown and syrupy. Drizzle a little jelly into cold water to test; if it is threadlike, then it is ready. Remove from the heat and pour into sterilized bottles.

Makes 4 to 5 cups

4 pounds *palayamkodan* bananas, peeled and sliced
3 cups water
3 cups sugar
4 tablespoons lemon juice

Ginger Lime Squash
Injiyum Naranga Paniyam

This lime concentrate has the sweet pungency of ginger and can be diluted with soda or water, then topped off with ice cubes for a cool summer drink. I have also stirred it into fresh chopped fruit salad and iced tea, and used it as a base for fruit punches. If lime is unavailable, use fresh lemon juice.

Mix the sugar and water in a deep pan, cover, and let sit overnight.

Stir the grated ginger into the sugar mixture and cook over medium heat for 8 to 10 minutes, until the sugar has completely dissolved.

Strain the mixture through a muslin cloth, put back in pan and place back on the heat. Cook until it forms a thick syrup of threadlike consistency or when a candy thermometer inserted in the liquid registers 215 degrees F. Remove from heat and add the lime or lemon juice while the syrup is still hot.

Cool and pour into sterilized bottles.

Makes 600 ml

12 cups sugar
3 cups water
3 tablespoons grated fresh ginger
2 cups lime or lemon juice

Black Coffee with Raw Cane Sugar

Kattan Kaapi

Fresh coffee brewed in a coffeemaker can be used, but this is the old-fashioned way—the coffee is steeped in a pot until the grounds settle. Then the thin decoction is poured out carefully. Raw cane sugar can be substituted with brown sugar or molasses; this adds a wholesome flavor to the coffee, which somehow seems to taste best when served in a glass. Some old-timers prefer to drink coffee in little ceramic bowls called kopas. *Start your day with a steaming hot glass of molasses coffee or serve with a Kerala breakfast or teatime snacks.*

Serves 4

¼ cup finely ground coffee beans
5 cups water
2 tablespoons raw cane sugar

Put the ground coffee beans in a heat-proof pitcher.

In a pot, bring the water to a boil and pour over the ground coffee beans. Cover immediately and steep for 10 minutes, or until the coffee grounds settle and the coffee decoction is clear of grounds.

Slowly pour the steeped coffee into a container, leaving the grounds at the bottom of the pitcher. Add the cane sugar to the coffee and stir well. Pour into glasses to serve.

Sweet Milky Tea

Chaya

Sweet Indian chai *has become popular, and any brand of strong tea can be used to make this refreshing drink. A spoon of ground ginger can be added when the tea is boiled for ginger tea, or a few pods of crushed cardamom can be added for cardamom tea. Visiting my daughter Rajni in New York, I was touched when she welcomed me with a cup of sweet milky Taj Mahal tea with Marie biscuits to dip in—this was a ritual we had shared for many years in India, and I felt at home immediately!* Like the molasses coffee, sweet milky tea can be served in little glasses, in true tea shop tradition, with a few biscuits to dip in.

Serves 4

2 cups water
3 cups milk
2 teaspoons strong Indian tea leaves
4 teaspoons sugar

In a medium pan, bring the water and milk to a boil. When it boils, add the tea leaves and remove from the heat. Add ginger or cardamom at this point, if desired. Cover with a lid.

Steep the tea for 1 minute and then strain into a teapot. Add the sugar, and serve.

Spices & Produce of Kerala

Breakfast of steamed rice cake, lace-rimmed pancakes, and stew, with the morning paper

Accompaniments (*clockwise from top left*) – fried bittergourd, dried prawn chutney, spiced buttermilk, shallot chutney, coconut chutney, coconut and curry leaf chutney powder

Curried Chickpeas (page 71)
Kadala Karri

Fish Roasted in Banana Leaves (page 80)
Meen Pollichathu

Shrimp Fry / *Chemmeen Olathiath* (page 96)

Left page: A vegetarian meal (*clockwise from top*) – mashed tapioca, string bean saute, red beans and pumpkin in coconut milk, cabbage with ground coconut, shallots with tamarind and roasted coconut, mixed vegetable curry

A Suriani Feast

Photographer: Igor Setar

Assorted Pickles

Steamed Banana Leaf Cakes (page 176)
Elayappam

Duck Roast (page 137)
Tharavu Roast

Fried Beef (page 106)
Erachi Olathiathu

Palahaarams
(*clockwise from top left*)
steamed rice batter cake, black halvah, banana chips, rosa cookies, sesame seed balls, roasted rice cones, savory rolls, fried molasses cakes, plantain fritters, sweet banana chips

(*center*)
steamed jackruit cones

Mung Bean Porridge / *Cherupayaru Payasam* (page 215)
served with yogurt, fruit and palm syrup

The pickle cupboard

The Best Toddy Shop in Kerala

The best toddy shop in Kerala can be found off Highway 47 on the road to Allepey. A potholed mud road leads through the marsh to a large shack perched on stilts near the edge of the water. A few houses spewing wood smoke are scattered along the way, each with a little yard fringed by coconut palms, drumstick trees, and tapioca shrubs. Little wooden gates keep the country hens from wandering out; instead they scratch about the dirt yards, watched by a few ducks and cats.

The best *kallu shaap* opens late in the morning. It is the "best" because the proprietor, M. Augustine, says so—on a white metal board above the door. The place is incongruously named Mulla Pandal (jasmine bower), although there is no hint of any flowers around. Instead, tall reeds grow thickly around the periphery of the shop. The shack is made of rough country wood with large, open palmleaf shutters all around it, propped open by poles. Inside, the room is large and airy. A few cracks in the wooden floor reveal glimpses of the shimmering water below. Small wooden tables with benches fill up the room. The walls are bare except for a picture of the communist leader Namboodiripad, and below it is a little wooden trellis with a cone of plastic flowers. M. Augustine has a desk at the entrance and is seated there as we enter. He is unfazed by our arrival. It is late in the afternoon and there are many regulars seated. After a cursory glance at us, they turn back to their glasses.

My husband, George, a few friends, and I are returning from a wedding. Their children—Aley and Sara, on vacation from college in America—are as curious as I am. The toddy shops that dot the countryside are famous for their delicious country fare and though there are many 'family' *kallu shaaps* where women and children can sit and enjoy the experience, we want the real thing.

Most toddy shops are licensed to sell the sour country brew that is freshly tapped each morning from coconut palms all over Kerala. The palm tree is prepared for tapping when the flowers ripen and are about to burst. The top of the flowering branch is lopped off and a thick paste of mud is applied, which helps the sap to rise to the surface. The sweet, milky liquid is then collected in mud pots that are inverted over the branch. Soon, the sap rises and starts filling up the pots that are emptied daily.

M. Augustine explains the process of procuring toddy to us while Aley takes notes for her journal and Sara shoots pictures to take back to America.

The shop deserves full marks for authentic atmosphere and ambience, we decide. The large open windows frame a picture-book view of the tranquil backwaters, fringed by the omnipresent coconut palms. In the distance we spy cormorants, and nearer, a flock of ducks skims the placid waters. Little canoes glide past with their passengers in crisp white *mundus* standing perfectly balanced, umbrellas in hand to shield them from the fierce afternoon sun. A large rice barge laden with coconut husks moves at a much slower pace. We peer down into the tiny makeshift kitchen at the rear where an earthen *chatti* simmers. Piquant, seductive aromas waft through the air and we are ravenous.

We sit at a table in a corner overlooking the backwaters and immediately jugs of sweet toddy and the headier fermented toddy are brought over. My husband, a connoisseur of authentic Kerala cooking, asks about the specials for the day. Quail and turtle meat *olathiathu*, we are told. We order one of everything they have in the kitchen including the specials and the food starts rolling in: little plates of crisp fried fish and shrimps, fiery red coccum-sour fish curry, spicy fried beef, and curried mashed tapioca. The delicious food is everything we had expected. Plates of *kada* and *aama erachi*, the specials of the day, are brought next. Anxious not to miss out on the whole *kallu shaap* experience, I put aside my squeamishness for unfamiliar foods and try both. The quail is crisp and perfectly cooked with spices, curry leaves, and sweet coconut oil. The turtle meat is also surprisingly good, though a bit rubbery like squid.

The Kerala Kitchen

The proprietor is jovial and anxious for us to have a good time. Knowledgeable about food and a good raconteur, he stands nearby answering our endless queries. He speaks about the fresh catch that was brought in that morning, the new road that is coming through, and his early student days with the Marxist party.

Our eyes are streaming now from the fiery food, but we cannot stop. We had eaten a hurried *biryani* lunch hours earlier at the wedding, but the smells and flavors of the food have whetted our appetites again. Aley asks the serving boy for water and he brings us more sweet toddy instead. "It is true," George says, "they do not serve water at *kallu shaaps*, so drink up." The toddy is fresh and barely fermented, and goes down smoothly like a fizzy soft drink. The men are drinking the fermented brew, headier than our sweet *kallu* and the two pitchers of toddy are constantly replenished. By now, we have also sampled little quail eggs, fried squid, and oysters, all cooked in the simple, easy fashion of country cooking. Shallots, curry leaves, coccum, pepper, chillis, coriander, and coconut in various sublime combinations give each dish its unique flavor.

Several pitcherfuls later, and after what seemed like a hundred plates of delectable tidbits, we are sated and moan, "*Madhi*" (enough)! We are pleasantly lightheaded and in high spirits, but not inebriated. This is truly the best *kallu shaap* in Kerala, in the world, we proclaim, as we make our happy way to the car.

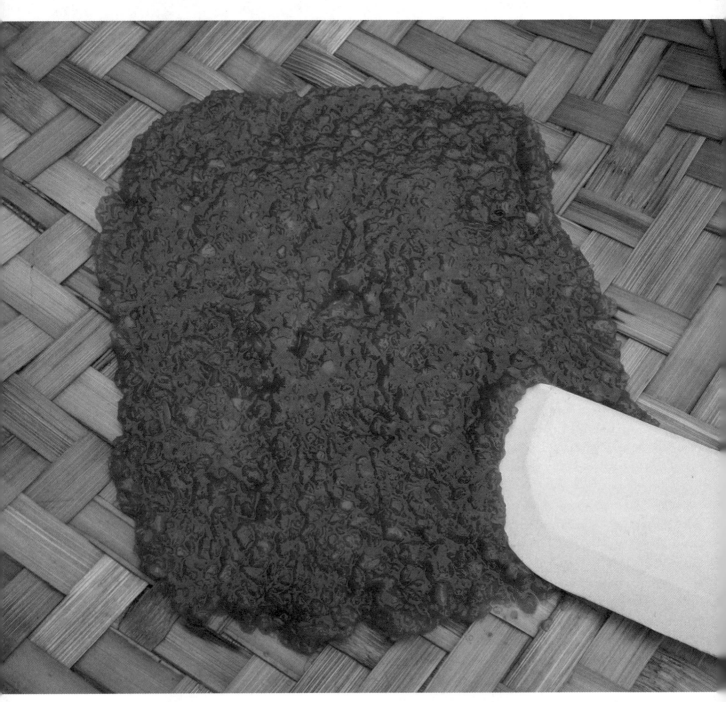

Thera (Mango and Rice Fruit Leather, page 184) drying in the sun

SWEET AND SAVORY SNACKS

Syrian Christian cuisine boasts of a wide range of *palahaarams* or sweet and savory snacks: hot plantain and lentil fritters and a variety of steamed rice cakes freshly made for the tea table; crisp rosa cookies, sweet and savory *cheedas* and *kozhalappams* stored away in old biscuit tins; syrupy cones of *churuttu*, halvahs, and mango fruit leather wrapped in parchment paper. *Palahaarams* are kept in the storeroom and taken out at tea-time or when guests arrive to pay their respects to a family elder, sometimes bringing an invitation to a wedding or christening.

Preparing *palahaarams* the old-fashioned way is a laborious task that very few attempt today. One must truly respect the home management and culinary skills of Syrian Christian housewives who until recent times managed large estate homes and farmhouses in Kerala with age-old techniques and few conveniences. The kitchens were buzzing with activity through the year. Rice was pounded the old-fashioned way and roasted in enormous *uralis* to produce the flour so essential for daily use, and also to be sent to sons and daughters in distant places. There was also the preparation of halvahs, banana chips to be fried and salted or sweetened with raw cane sugar, fruit leather to be made with the baskets of mangoes in the storeroom, and ripe jackfruit to be stirred into a thick preserve.

Growing up in Bombay, my mother was unrelenting in her efforts to keep us connected with Kerala. She would have hot *palahaarams* on the table for tea when we arrived home from school, *pidis* (steamed fistfuls of dough) or boiled sweet potato to dip into coconut, rice flakes sweetened with cane sugar, leaf cakes hot off the griddle, and a special treat—hot plantain fritters—if there was a supply of plantains from Kerala. Though we often grumbled, asking why we could not have cakes and biscuits like the other kids in the neighborhood, I eventually developed a passion for *avalos podi*, *neyappam*, and all the other teatime snacks I had once scorned.

Roasted and unroasted rice flour, jaggery (raw cane sugar), plantains, and even prepared *palahaarams* are available at ethnic food stores in the United States. However, if you have a yearning for the real homemade flavor of traditional Syrian Christian snacks, the following recipes (chosen from a vast repertoire) are authentic, with some modifications that attempt to simplify the sometimes arduous methods of old.

Rosa Cookies

Achappam

These crisp fried cookies are named after the flowery designs of the iron achappam *mold. This popular recipe is derived from the cookbooks of the early Dutch merchant families who arrived in Kochi in the fifteenth century. Most bakeries in Kerala sell packaged rosa cookies, but they cannot be compared with fresh homemade cookies.*

In a large bowl, mix all of the ingredients except the eggs and oil, using enough water to make a thin batter. Add the well-beaten eggs and mix thoroughly.

Heat the oil in a wok or deep pot. Dip the mold in the hot oil until it is well-heated; dip the mold into the batter until it is three-quarters submerged; then dip it again into the hot oil. The lacy cookie should detach from the mold. When the lacy cookie detaches, again dip the mold into the batter and then into the oil, repeating the process so you have about 5 cookies in each batch. Continue frying cookies for 1 minute or until they turn light brown, flipping them over once.

Repeat this process to make more cookies, frying each batch until they are crisp and golden. Drain the cookies on paper towels and store in airtight containers once they have cooled.

Makes 30 to 40

4 cups roasted rice flour
2 cups thick coconut milk
2 tablespoons sugar
2 teaspoons sesame seeds
¼ teaspoon ground nutmeg
Pinch of salt
Water, as needed
2 eggs, beaten well
Oil for deep-frying

Equipment: *achappam* cookie mold

Sweet Host Rolls
Hosti Kozhallappam

I am told that my aunt Rosakutty concocted the recipe for these delightfully airy cookies. She passed it on to the unemployed women of her parish who soon found this a lucrative business. These delicate wafers rolled into cookie rolls are prepared in the mold used to prepare communion hosts. A pizzelle maker is an adequate substitute if you cannot get your hands on an authentic host mold.

Sift the flour several times until very fine.

In a large bowl, mix all the ingredients (except the ghee or butter), making sure that there are no lumps. The batter should be thin and smooth.

Heat the host mold slightly and brush with ghee or butter. Pour in a tablespoon of batter, and swirl until it coats the mold completely. Press the mold shut and hold over medium heat, heating each side for 1 to 2 minutes. Remove the cookie from the mold, and roll it quickly around a ½-inch-thick wooden stick to form a slim roll.

Continue making more rolls in this way, rolling each while still hot. Store the host rolls in airtight containers once they have cooled.

Makes 40

4 cups all-purpose flour
2 eggs
½ cup powdered sugar
4 cups milk
1 tablespoon ghee or butter

Equipment: host cookie mold or pizzelle maker

Savory Rolls

Kozhalappam

This is made with a spicy dough of rice flour, coconut, and spices pressed into thin rolls and fried crisp. The kozhalappams can also be coated with a light sugar syrup, the sweet frost complementing the spicy flavor of the crisp rolls. Once they have cooled, the rolls must be stored in airtight containers.

Mix the rice flour with the grated coconut in a mixing bowl. Knead lightly to remove lumps and set aside for an hour.

Grind the shallots, garlic, and cumin seeds to a fine paste. In a small bowl, mix this paste into the coconut milk along with the salt.

Put the rice flour mixture in a heavy pot and cook over low heat for 3 minutes, stirring constantly to prevent the mixture from burning. Add the coconut milk mixture and continue stirring for 2 minutes or until steam rises.

Remove from heat and add the sesame seeds and just enough water to make a soft dough. Set aside, covered with a damp cloth for an hour.

Form 1-inch balls with the dough and press between waxed paper or banana leaves. Roll each ball of dough into thin 4-inch rounds. Roll each circle around the oiled handle of a wooden spoon. Press the overlapping edges together and slip off the handle.

Once the dough is prepared, heat the oil in a deep pot. Deep-fry the rolls in batches in the hot oil until crisp and light brown in color. Drain on paper towels. Cool and store in airtight containers.

Makes 24

2½ cups fine unroasted rice flour
1 cup grated fresh coconut
6 shallots
3 cloves garlic
½ teaspoon cumin seeds
½ cup thick coconut milk
½ teaspoon salt
1 tablespoon sesame seeds
Water, as needed
Oil for deep-frying

Frosted Doughballs

Cheedas

*These crisp balls of fried rice dough are coated with a
nutmeg-flavored sugar frosting.*

Sift the rice flour three times with the salt into a mixing bowl.

In the mixing bowl, knead the butter into the rice
flour. Add the eggs, coconut milk, and cumin, and knead
lightly until the mixture becomes a soft dough. Add
more flour if necessary.

Roll the dough into marble-size balls. Press each ball
on the back of a fork, flattening it until it forms a little
disk. Roll the disk to form a ridged cylinder.

While the *cheeda* rolls are being prepared, heat the oil
in a deep pot. Lower the heat and fry the *cheeda* in
batches for 2 to 3 minutes, until they are crisp and a
light brown color. Transfer to a tray as they are cooked.

PREPARE THE FROSTING:

In a small pan, boil the water and sugar until it forms
a thick syrup. Put a few drops on a plate and then test by
pressing it between your thumb and forefinger; if it
forms sticky threads then it is ready. Add the nutmeg or
cinnamon and remove immediately from the heat.

Pour the frosting over the fried *cheedas*, stirring and
tossing to prevent lumps. Spread on the tray, and cool
until the *cheedas* are white and frosty.

Store the *cheedas* in airtight containers.

Makes 1½ pounds

4 cups rice flour
1 teaspoon salt
2 tablespoons butter
2 eggs, beaten
2 cups thick coconut milk
1 teaspoon ground cumin
Oil for deep-frying

FROSTING:
1 cup water
1 cup plus 2 tablespoons sugar
½ teaspoon ground nutmeg or cinnamon

Roasted Rice and Coconut Powder

Avalos Podi

Avalos podi *is a roasted rice and coconut mixture that is a base for several sweet preparations. Many a child bound for boarding school had a tin of* avalos podi *mixed with sugar in her tuck box, which she brought out for midnight feasts, or to sneak a spoonful of memories from at tea-time.*

In a large bowl, soak the rice in water to cover for 2 hours; drain and dry in the sun. Grind the dry rice to a powder in a grinder and sift to remove any lumps.

Mix the rice flour and grated coconut in a large mixing bowl until it has a coarse crumbly texture. Add the cumin seeds and salt and mix again. Shape the mixture in a mound, cover, and set aside for 3 hours.

Dry-roast the rice mixture in a heavy-bottomed skillet for 15 to 20 minutes, stirring continuously, until it is an even, golden color. Cool and grind again if there are any lumps. Store the powder in airtight containers. (See recipes using *avalos podi* on pages 169–171.)

Makes 1½ pounds

5 cups uncooked rice
2 cups grated fresh coconut
½ teaspoon cumin seeds
½ teaspoon salt

Roasted Rice Balls

Avalos Oonda

These grainy balls are made with avalos podi *and held together with a thin sugar syrup. A perfect syrup is the key to rice balls that crumble in your mouth—and not before. If the syrup is overcooked, the rice balls become hard—veritable jawbreakers.*

Mix the water, sugar, and lime juice in a deep pan, cover, and store overnight.

Bring the mixture to a boil and cook until it reaches 1 thread consistency. Test with a candy thermometer—when the syrup reaches 215 degrees F it is ready. Add the ghee and remove from the heat. Add the cardamom powder.

In a bowl, mix the warm sugar syrup with the *avalos podi* and roll into little 1-inch balls. Roll the balls in dry *avalos podi*, and place on a tray to dry. Store in airtight containers when cool.

Makes 25 to 30

½ cup water
1 cup sugar
1 tablespoon lime juice
1 tablespoon melted ghee
½ teaspoon ground cardamom
2 cups *avalos podi* plus more for rolling (page 168)

Roasted Rice Cones

Churuttu

These cones of syrupy avalos podi *encased in wafer thin pastry are a traditional Syrian Christian sweet. It was almost impossible to get the recipe for this labor-intensive snack; no one, I was told, made it at home any more. Then, Annamma, my sister's mother-in-law, produced an authentic recipe using rice flour for the* mandaka (pastry) *and* paani (palm syrup). *An old-school cook and a gracious hostess with years of experience in running a large estate home, she does not believe in shortcuts. With her team of domestic helpers, her kitchens hum with activity: jams and pickles prepared with fresh produce from the estate, rice flour powdered and roasted in large* uralis *to be sent to her children, and* palahaarams (snacks) *for her own storeroom and for the family.*

So, for the purist, here is the recipe for homemade churuttu *made from scratch, using sugar syrup instead of* paani *as the latter may be unavailable. However, it requires an extra pair of hands to help prepare and cook the pastry before it dries out!*

Makes 48

MANDAKA (PASTRY):

6 cups unroasted rice flour, sieved three times
2½ to 3 cups hot water
1 large banana leaf, washed and wilted over a
    hot flame

FILLING:

3 cups water
5 cups sugar
2 tablespoons lime or lemon juice
8 cups *avalos podi* (page 168)

PREPARE THE PASTRY:

Put the rice flour in a mixing bowl, make a well in the center, and pour the hot water into it. Mix and knead the flour into a stiff pastry dough.

Form the dough into smooth ¾-inch balls. Roll each ball of pastry into a wafer-thin round, and cut to measure 5 inches in diameter. Dust the rounds with flour on one side only, so the pastry does not dry out.

Place the wilted banana leaf in a deep pot. Lightly cook the pastry rounds on a medium hot griddle for just 30 seconds on each side. The pastry must still be limp. Stack the pastries in the pot with the banana leaf as they are cooked, covering them with the loose end of the leaf as each round is added. When all the pastry rounds are cooked, keep them wrapped in the banana leaf parcel as you prepare the filling to keep the pastry soft and pliable.

Bring the water to a boil in a deep pan; add the sugar, stirring until it dissolves. Cook the syrup until it reaches 1 thread consistency, then add the lime juice. Set aside 3 tablespoons of syrup. Add the *avalos podi* to the remaining syrup and mix well.

Cut each round of pastry in half and wet the edges of each half with the reserved syrup. Shape each semi-circle into a cone with the dry side facing inside, leaving one end of the pastry free to close. Stuff each cone with 1½ tablespoons of stuffing. Cover the tops and seal the edges. Place on a tray. Continue until all the *churuttu* are prepared. Set aside for 2 hours, until the syrup from the filling has moistened and seeped into the pastry.

Stack the *churuttu* carefully in an airtight container and store until needed.

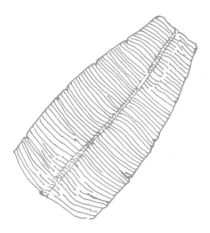

Sweet Rice Flakes

Aval Vilayichathu

Brown unpolished or polished rice is soaked in water, sun-dried, and hand-pounded until each grain is flattened to produce beaten rice flakes, also known as aval *or* poha. *The jaggery or raw cane sugar that is used here can be replaced with brown sugar.*

My mother always had a tin of aval vilayichathu *stored away and, though it is delicious eaten as a sweet dry mixture, I loved it best with mashed banana.*

In a medium skillet, heat the ghee and fry the sesame seeds and chickpeas until crisp, but do not brown. Set aside.

In a large pot, melt the jaggery in the water and heat over medium heat. When it starts boiling, add the grated coconut and stir continuously over low heat for 5 minutes. When the water has almost evaporated and the syrup is thick, remove from the heat and allow to cool.

Once the mixture is cool, add the rice flakes and chickpea mixture. Mix well. Add the cardamom powder and cool completely before storing in an airtight container.

Makes 1 pound

¼ cup ghee, melted
½ cup black sesame seeds
1 cup roasted split chickpeas
3 cups jaggery or brown sugar
2½ cups water
1 pound grated fresh coconut
8 cups rice flakes
1 teaspoon ground cardamom

Fistfuls

Pidis

This is my mother's recipe for the fist-shaped steamed rice cakes that we dipped into sugar or ate with shallot and chilli chutney. Often, the pidis *would be in the varying sizes of the assortment of fists that shaped these little cakes: from my baby niece Anila's tiny palm to a visiting cousin's larger hand. Serve with sugar, honey, or a shallot and chilli chutney.*

Heat the water in a pot and add the oil. Lower the heat and add the rice flour, salt, and sugar. Mix vigorously with a wooden spoon for 2 minutes to remove any lumps. Remove from the heat, and add the grated coconut as you continue mixing. Set aside until lukewarm.

Grease your palms before you start working with the dough. Shape the dough into lime-size balls, place each ball in your fist and clench tight. Unclench the fist and remove the dough, which is now marked with the indentations from your fingers.

Bring water to a boil in the bottom of a steamer. Place all the prepared *pidis* in the steamer tray and steam for 10 minutes or until they are firm.

Makes 12

4 cups water
1 teaspoon oil
2 cups unroasted rice flour, sifted
½ teaspoon salt
½ teaspoon sugar
½ cup grated fresh coconut

VARIATION: This dough can also be used to make a sweet or savoury flatbread called *orotti* which is from Thalassery in Northern Kerala. Add 1 tablespoon of sugar for a sweet snack; or add green chilli paste for a savoury vegan bread to accompany a curry. To make, divide the dough while still warm into lime-sized balls and press onto an oiled surface to form round circles; roast on both sides on a pan till done.

Steamed Rice Balls
Kozhukottai

In this recipe, kozhukottai *are stuffed with minced jackfruit. But they can also be stuffed with a sweet coconut and raisin filling, mango or pineapple pulp, or any prepared seasonal fruit purée mixed with grated coconut.* Serve hot or cold.

In a medium pot, cook the minced jackfruit with the sugar for 5 minutes or until it is thick; add the ground nutmeg and set aside to cool. Once it is cool, add the coconut to the jackfruit pulp and divide the mixture into eight portions.

Bring the water a boil in a medium pot, lower the heat, and add the oil, salt, and rice flour. Knead the flour mixture into a smooth, firm dough. Remove from the heat, knead again, and set aside until lukewarm.

Divide the dough into eight balls of equal size. Press each ball of dough in the palm of your hand to form a cup, place a portion of the jackfruit mixture in it, and seal. Smooth and form each into a ball.

Bring water to boil in the bottom of a steamer. Stack the rice balls in a steamer tray and steam for 20 minutes.

Makes 8

1 cup minced jackfruit
¼ cup sugar
½ teaspoon ground nutmeg
½ cup grated fresh coconut
2 cups water
1 teaspoon oil
¼ teaspoon salt
1 cup fine unroasted rice flour

Sweet Steamed Rice Cake

Vattayappam

In Kerala, toddy is used to prepare this sweet, spongy steamed cake, but dry or fresh yeast can be substituted. This recipe has been modified from the traditional, and is by far the best of the many recipes for vattayappam. *My sister-in-law Ancy also makes a delicate unleavened* appam *similar to* vattayappam, *using a thin batter of rice flour, coconut milk, and sugar. The steamed cakes are sliced into delicious thin slivers.* Cut into quarters and serve with honey or paani. Vattayappam *can be kept for a few days, refrigerated, and can be frozen as well.*

Mix the fine rice flour and yeast in a deep mixing bowl.

Bring the water to a boil and mix with the coarse rice flour to make a thin gruel. Set aside to cool to lukewarm.

When the gruel has cooled down and is just warm enough to raise the yeast, add to the yeast mixture. Add the coconut milk and sugar and leave to rise in a warm place for an hour or longer.

When the batter has risen, stir in the raisins and cardamom. Pour into two 8-inch greased pans.

Bring water to a boil in the bottom of a steamer and steam the cakes for 12 minutes or until they are firm.

Makes 2

2 cups fine unroasted rice flour, sifted three times
1 teaspoon active dry yeast
2 cups water
½ cup coarse rice flour or cream of wheat
½ cup thick coconut milk
½ cup sugar
¼ cup raisins
4 cardamom pods, crushed

Steamed Banana Leaf Cakes

Elayappam

Every home in Kerala has a few banana trees that have a multitude of uses—here, they provide the leaves that give this cake its name. A simply prepared teatime snack, leaf cakes can be kept refrigerated for up to a week.

Bring the water to a boil in a large pot, lower the heat, and add the oil, salt, and rice flour. Quickly knead to a fine paste, removing any lumps as you work the dough. Remove from the heat and let it cool slightly. While still warm, divide the dough into eight portions and set aside.

Mix the coconut, jaggery, and cardamom, and divide into eight portions.

Press a portion of rice dough on each leaf or parchment square until it is an even 3-inch square. Spread a portion of the coconut mixture on one half of each rice dough square and fold the leaves over. Pinch along the sides of the pastry until the filling is well-sealed.

When the leaf cakes are all prepared, stack them in a steamer tray and steam for 15 to 20 minutes. Set aside for an hour and serve warm or cold.

Makes 8

1 cup water
1 teaspoon oil
¼ teaspoon salt
1 cup roasted rice flour
2 cups grated fresh coconut
1 cup jaggery or brown sugar
½ teaspoon coarsely crushed cardamom seeds
8 (4-inch) squares of banana leaves or parchment paper

Plantain and Coconut Sauté

Ethakka Vilayachathu

This is a recipe from my grandmother Mamikutty, and a family favorite. My favorite comfort food, this sweet dish evokes happy memories of rainy evenings in Bombay. Serve hot or cold.

Heat the ghee in a pan with a heavy base, over low to medium heat. Add the cardamom pods, sauté for a few seconds, then add the ripe plantain slices. Stir gently so the plantains do not break. Add the sugar and continue cooking till the plantains start to caramelize. At this stage, stir in the coconut and raisins, gently stirring to loosen the browned parts in the pan. The plantains should be browned and each slice coated with the caramelized coconut and raisin mixture.

Serves 4

½ cup ghee or butter
4 cardamom pods, crushed
6 ripe plantains, peeled and sliced into
    ¼-inch rounds
½ cup sugar
1 cup grated fresh coconut
¼ cup raisins

Fried Plantain Fritters

Ethakka Appam

Introduced to Kerala by the Portuguese, plantains, also known as nendrikkai *or* ethakka, *are a favorite food of all Malayalis. As it is easily digested and highly nutritious, steamed plantain or dried plantain flour porridge is often one of the first solid foods that infants in Kerala are fed.*

These crisp plantain fritters—delicious but less wholesome—are also known as pazham bajji *and are sold in tea shops across Kerala.*

In a small bowl mix the rice flour, sugar, baking powder, salt, and enough water to make a thick batter.

Heat the oil in a deep skillet. Dip the plantain pieces in the batter and fry in batches until crisp and golden. Drain on paper towels and serve hot.

Makes 24

½ cup rice flour
3 tablespoons sugar
½ teaspoon baking powder
¼ teaspoon salt
Water as needed
Oil for deep-frying
4 ripe plantains, each halved crosswise and then
  each half cut lengthwise into 3 slices

Fried Plantain Balls

Unnakai

Borrowed from the Muslim community of Malabar, these steamed and mashed plantain balls are stuffed with a mixture of coconut and raisins that make them especially delicious. Serve hot as a teatime snack.

Makes 12 to 15

1 cup grated fresh coconut
1 teaspoon sugar
¼ cup raisins
1 teaspoon ground cardamom
6 ripe plantains, steamed for 5 minutes
Oil for deep-frying

In a small bowl, mix the coconut, sugar, raisins, and cardamom and set aside.

Peel the plantains and slice in half lengthwise. Remove the center vein with seeds. Mash the plantains and form into lime-size balls. Shape the balls into little cups in the palm of your hand. Stuff each with 1 tablespoon of the coconut mixture, close, and seal. Shape the stuffed balls until they are smooth and round.

Heat the oil in a deep skillet. Fry the plantain balls in the hot oil in batches. Remove as they turn golden brown and drain on paper towels.

Plantain Chips

Kai Varathathu

Raw plantain thinly sliced directly into a huge cauldron of boiling oil, surfacing crisp and golden is a familiar sight in plantain stalls throughout Kerala. Delicious hot or cold, these can be stored for months.

Makes 1 to 1½ pounds

1 tablespoon salt
3 tablespoons water
Oil for deep-frying
6 raw plantains, peeled and sliced into thin rounds

In a small bowl, mix the water and salt and set aside.

Heat the oil in a deep pot. Add the plantain slices in batches and fry until crisp and golden, stirring the oil occasionally so the chips are evenly cooked. Sprinkle a little salt solution into the oil before removing the chips with a slotted spoon. Drain in a deep colander or basket.

Spread the chips out on trays to cool and then store in airtight tins.

Sweet Plantain Chips

Ethakka Sarkara Puratti

These little wedges of ginger-and-jaggery-flavored plaintain chips can be stored for months. I have also tried this recipe with fresh fruit wedges—to be served immediately as a dessert.

Makes 1 pound

Oil for deep-frying
4 large plantains, sliced in ¼-inch-wide semicircles
½ teaspoon salt
2 cups jaggery or brown sugar
½ cup water
½ teaspoon ground ginger
½ teaspoon ground cumin
2 teaspoons roasted rice flour

Heat the oil in a deep pot. Deep-fry the plantain slices for 2 to 3 minutes, until lightly browned. As they are cooked remove the chips from the oil and sprinkle with a little salt. Set the fried chips aside.

In a wide, shallow pan, mix the jaggery and water and melt over low heat until it becomes a thick syrup. Stir in the ginger and cumin. Put the chips into the syrup and stir until they are evenly coated with the syrup. Remove from the heat.

Sprinkle with the rice flour and cool completely before storing.

Black Halvah

Karruthu Halvah

Halvahs, an import from the Middle East, have been adapted to native tastes and a wide range of halvahs are prepared with local produce. A halvah maker from Kerala would take soft, fudgy black halvah along with pumpkin and milk halvahs around to Malayali homes in Bombay. They were made fresh in his kitchen, he told us, in a huge urali *that he had brought over from Kerala many years before. He would hand us each a sliver to taste as he carefully weighed the thick squares of halvah.*

Black halvah is made with fine cake flour, coconut milk, and raw cane sugar which is cooked into a thick, dark fudge in a heavy-bottomed vessel. The halvah must be stirred constantly over low heat for 2 to 4 hours and must never be left unattended. Halvah should be wrapped in parchment paper or plastic wrap before storing away in airtight containers. Cut it into thin slices to serve.

Put the flour in a very large mixing bowl with 2 cups of the water. Knead well to make a soft dough. Add another 18 cups of the water to the dough to make a thin batter. Strain the batter through a thin muslin cloth and set aside for 2 hours. When the floury sediment settles to the bottom, drain the clear water from the top of the batter.

Dissolve the jaggery in a separate bowl with the remaining 3 cups of water; set aside for an hour and then strain.

Put the flour batter in a large, heavy-bottomed pot. Add the jaggery mixture, sugar, and coconut milk, and stir until it looks like a thick, milky gruel. Heat to a boil over high heat stirring continuously, and once the mixture starts boiling, lower the heat. Simmer for 1 to 1½ hours, stirring and turning the mix continuously until it has thickened. Add the butter, cashews and cardamom and cook for 20 to 30 more minutes, as you continue stirring.

When the halvah mix is dark—almost black—and has cooked to a thick fudge, pour into a greased 9 x 13-inch baking dish, smoothing the surface with the back of a spoon. Allow the halvah to cool and then cut into large squares for storage.

Makes 1¼ pounds

4 cups fine cake flour
23 cups water, plus more as needed
14 cups jaggery or dark brown sugar
½ cup sugar
6 cups thick coconut milk
1 cup butter or ghee
1 cup fresh cashews, halved
½ teaspoon ground cardamom

Jackfruit Halvah
Chakka Halvah

This is a soft halvah that does not slice as well as the other halvahs. Like all halvahs, it must be stirred continuously while cooking (about 1 hour). Cut into large squares and store in parchment paper.

Steam the jackfruit pods, chop into pieces, and purée in a food processor.

Put the puréed jackfruit in a large, heavy-bottomed open pot. Add the milk, jaggery, water, and half the ghee to the puréed fruit. Mix well and place over high heat. When it starts boiling, lower the heat and add the remaining butter. Simmer, stirring continuously, for about 1 hour.

Add the cashews and cardamom and continue cooking for 25 to 30 minutes. Remove the halvah from the heat when the mixture turns into a thick mass. Pour into a greased 9 x 13-inch baking dish and spread evenly, smoothing the top with a spoon.

Allow the halvah to cool and then cut into large squares and store in an airtight container.

Makes ¾ pound

30 ripe jackfruit pods, seeded
1 cup milk
2 cups jaggery or dark brown sugar
½ cup water
1 cup ghee or butter
½ cup cashews, halved
1 teaspoon cardamom powder

Milk Halvah

Paal Halvah

This is a delicious, soft, fudgy halvah made of milk and wheat. As with all halvahs, cut it into large squares and store, wrapped in parchment paper or plastic wrap.

Makes 1½ pounds

In a large bowl, mix 2 cups of the water with the flour to make a soft dough. Add the remaining 15 cups water, mix well, and strain through a thin muslin cloth discarding any sediment left in cloth.

Put the flour mixture, sugar, and milk in a large, heavy pot, and place over high heat. When it starts boiling, lower the heat and simmer for 1 to 1½ hours, stirring continuously. Add the ghee gradually as the halvah thickens.

When the halvah mixture has cooked to a thick fudgy mass and pulls away from the sides of the pot, add the lime juice and cardamom and stir well.

Remove from the heat and pour into a 9 x 13-inch greased dish, smoothing the surface with a spoon. Allow the halvah to cool and then cut into large squares.

17 cups water, plus more as needed
3 cups all-purpose flour
6 cups sugar
10 cups milk
2 cups ghee
2 tablespoons lime juice
½ teaspoon ground cardamom

Mango and Rice Fruit Leather

Thera

Thera *is a special sweet of late summer when there is an abundance of mangoes and the air is hot and dry before the monsoon. This is prepared over the course of days and spread on woven mats, giving it its characteristic trellis design (see photo on page 162). My mother-in-law, Kunjannamma, made* thera *every summer with the meticulous detail that made hers the best I have eaten. She would wrap each rectangle individually in cellophane.*

Be warned, thera *should only be attempted during dry, sunny weather, and must be meticulously attended to for good results. Of course, an easier but somehow less soul-satisfying method is at hand—oven-drying in place of sun-drying.*

Makes 48 to 50

24 cups thick mango purée
2 cups sugar
3 cups roasted rice flour

Equipment: A large woven reed mat, scrubbed
   clean

Strain the mango purée into a large pot and mix with the sugar. Warm over low heat just until the sugar has dissolved. Set aside to cool.

Divide the mango purée into three equal portions. Mix one portion with 2 cups of the rice flour. Reserve the rest of the mango purée in the refrigerator.

Place a large woven mat on a sunny terrace. Take half of the mango-rice paste and spread a thin layer on the mat in a large square or rectangle. (Place the other half covered in the refrigerator.) Leave the mat in direct sun to dry (this might take days), protecting it if necessary from birds and insects with netting.

When the paste has dried, spread the remaining half of the mango-rice paste directly over the first and set out to dry again. Dry the layers thoroughly, even if it takes days for each layer to dry.

When the first batch of *thera* is dry, prepare the second batch with the remaining 1 cup of rice flour and another portion of mango purée. Spread half of this over the earlier layers and allow to dry. Then spread the remaining mango-rice mixture over and allow this to dry.

Once this has also dried, spread a layer of the last batch of mango purée without any added rice flour. Dry as usual in the sun, and continue layering and drying until the mango purée is used up. The *thera* should be about ½-inch thick by now. Continue to dry in the sun until completely firm.

Cut the *thera* into 1×3-inch rectangles, peel off the mat, and wrap individually or store in airtight containers.

NOTE: To make perfect *thera* it is important not to rush the layering process. Each layer should be spread on as thinly as possible with a spatula or pastry brush to get perfectly layered bars of this delicious sweet.

Molasses Fritters

Neyappam

There are some foods, I am told, that must be prepared the old-fashioned way, and this classic Kerala snack is one of them even though they take several days to make. These fritters get their Malayalam name, Neyappam, *from the* neyu *(ghee or clarified butter) that is used in the original recipe. These will keep for up to 2 weeks refrigerated.*

In a large bowl, soak the rice in water to cover for 12 hours. Drain and allow to air dry. Once the rice is dry, grind it to a fine flour. Put the rice flour in a large mixing bowl. Mix the jaggery with the flour. Set aside for 2 days in an earthenware pot, covered with a thin muslin cloth, until it softens to a fine powder.

Two days later, heat the ghee in a skillet and fry the sesame seeds until lightly browned. Remove the seeds and set aside. Then fry the coconut slivers in the same ghee until they are a golden brown. Remove and set aside. Fry the onions in the same ghee until they are browned and crisp. Cool and crush to a fine powder.

Stir the rice mixture and add the ghee, fried sesame seeds, and coconut slivers, onion powder, cocnut milk, and salt. Mix well and set aside for 2 hours.

Add the ginger, cumin, and cardamom to the batter and stir well. It should be thick—the consistency of pancake batter.

Pour enough oil in a *neyappam* mold to cover the depressions, and place over high heat. When the oil is boiling, ladle some of the batter into each hole of the mold until it is filled to the brim. The *neyappams* should be covered by the oil with a little to spare. Lower the heat, and cook each batch for 3 to 5 minutes or until they turn a dark brown. Remove and set aside. Fry the remaining *neyappams*, adding and heating the oil each time you add more batter.

Makes 18 to 20

1 pound uncooked rice
½ pound jaggery or dark brown sugar
¼ cup ghee
1 tablespoon sesame seeds
¼ cup fresh coconut slivers
½ cup sliced onion
2 cups thick coconut milk
½ teaspoon salt
¼ teaspoon ground ginger
¼ teaspoon ground cumin
¼ teaspoon ground cardamom
Oil or ghee for deep-frying

Equipment: A cast-iron *neyappam* mold (see note on page 187)

Transfer the hot oil to a deep skillet, adding more oil if necessary, and fry all the *neyappams* until crisp. Set aside the fried *neyappams* in an earthenware pot for 3 hours before serving.

NOTE: If you do not have a *neyappam* mold, the batter can also be scooped in a large tablespoon or an ice cream scoop and deep-fried directly in hot oil.

Molasses Fritters—the Easy Method
Neyappam

Mix all the ingredients except the oil in a mixing bowl until they are well-blended.

Heat the oil in a wok and drop large rounded scoops of the batter into the hot oil. Lower the heat and turn over the dough after 2 minutes as it swells up and darkens to a deep brown. Remove from the oil and drain on paper towels.

½ pound rice flour
1 cup raw cane sugar
1 cup thick coconut milk
1 cup mashed banana
¼ cup ghee
¼ teaspoon ground cardamom
¼ teaspoon ground cumin
1 teaspoon baking powder
Oil for deep-frying

Lentil Fritters

Parippu Vada

These savory fritters (shaped like flying saucers) are sold in tea shops all over Kerala and are best eaten hot with coconut chutney.

Soak the pigeon peas in water for 4 hours. Drain and grind to a coarse paste with a mortar and pestle or food processor.

Put the ground pigeon peas in a mixing bowl and add all the remaining ingredients except for the oil.

Heat the oil in a deep pot. As the oil heats, shape the pea mixture into lime-size balls. Press each ball into disks with the center thick and tapered at the edges.

Fry in batches over low heat until crisp and golden brown. Drain on paper towels.

Makes 12

1 cup dried split pigeon peas
½ cup sliced shallots
1 tablespoon chopped green chillis
1 teaspoon minced fresh ginger
6 curry leaves, chopped
½ teaspoon asafoetida
1 teaspoon salt
Oil for deep-frying

Steamed Jackfruit Cones

Kumbilappam

The fragrant vazhana *(bog) leaves that are traditionally used to steam* kumbilappam *may be replaced by banana leaves or even parchment paper. The* vazhana *leaves give their aroma to these delectable little parcels. If they are not available, add grated nutmeg to the dough for flavor. Cool for an hour in the leafy cones, opening each just before eating. They will keep for up to a week in the refrigerator.*

In a medium pot, cook the jackfruit with the jaggery until thick.

Mix all the ingredients except the leaves to form a soft dough.

Prepare a steamer tall enough that all the cones can be stacked vertically.

Shape the leaves or parchment paper into little cones. Fill each cone with spoonfuls of the dough, tucking the tip of the leaf over to secure. Place upright in the steamer and cook for 20 minutes.

Makes 16

1 cup coarsely puréed jackfruit
¾ cup jaggery or brown sugar
1 cup fine unroasted rice flour
1 cup grated fresh coconut, coarsely ground
¼ teaspoon salt
16 *vazhana* leaves or 2½-inch semicircles of
   parchment paper

Sweet Mung Bean Fritters
Sukhiyan

A delicious tea-time snack or dessert made with cooked mung beans, jaggery, and coconut. Though the recipe calls for deep frying, sukhiyan *can also be steamed, making it a healthier choice. Both versions are delicious. Serve with a cup of tea or coffee.*

Cook the mung beans in the water and salt for 15 minutes on high heat till soft. Drain excess water and set aside until the mung beans have cooled down but are still warm.

Mash the warm mung beans well, slowly adding the grated jaggery, coconut, ground cardamom seeds, cumin powder, and ghee. When the mix has completely blended, shape into 1½-inch balls and set aside to cool completely.

PREPARE THE BATTER:
Mix the two flours, turmeric powder, and salt, and gradually add water till you get the consistency of thin crepe batter.

Heat some oil in a deep pan for frying. Test the oil with a drop of batter—it should rise quickly to the surface. Dip each mung ball into the batter and drop into the oil, frying 3 or 4 with each batch so they do not stick together. Turn gently to cook evenly. The batter will cook quickly, but do not brown the sukhiyan. Remove when done. Sukhiyan can be eaten hot or cold.

Makes XX

1 cup mung beans, soaked for 3 hours
3 cups water
¼ teaspoon salt
½ cup jaggery, finely grated
½ cup grated coconut
½ teaspoon ground cardamom seeds
1 teaspoon cumin powder
1 teaspoon ghee (optional)
Oil for frying

BATTER
½ cup flour
¼ cup fine rice flour
¼ teaspoon turmeric powder
¼ teaspoon salt
¼ cup water

VARIATION: For a healthier steamed version of *Sukhiyan*, mix a cup of flour, salt, and just enough water to make a smooth dough. Coat with a teaspoon of oil and set aside to rest. After an hour, knead and roll the dough into thin circles. Place a ball of sweetened mung beans in the center of each circle and pinch together to form a smooth ball. Steam for 15 minutes till the dough is transluscent.

PICKLES

Any meal in Kerala is incomplete without a few bowls of choice pickles. Pickles are made to preserve and enjoy seasonal produce for many months to come. If prepared well, a pickle will keep for several years. An array of pickles is always kept in stock for daily use and for special functions, and no storeroom in a Syrian Christian kitchen is complete without a few jars of salted mangoes, limes, or smoked gooseberries. A variety of pickles are prepared in most Kerala homes, with vegetables, meats, fish, and any seasonal produce that is available. The recipes are endless and are handed down over generations.

Summer is the ideal time for pickle making, as pickling requires hot, sunny days for drying the ingredients. *Baranis* (ceramic pickling jars) and bottles are washed in hot water and put out on sunny terraces where they dry in the hot summer sun. Mangoes—small and tender, salted or whole—are diced in large chunks or sliced into fine slivers, sun-dried, and then cooked with oil, vinegar, and a blend of spices. Tiny, tart limes, bitter gooseberries, and the many sour berries and fruits that grow abundantly on farms and estates are salted and dried to remove their bitterness and then spiced and pickled. Tiny shrimps, clams, and mussels, as well as fish of all kinds are also pickled in oils and spices. Beef, pork, chicken, and game make excellent pickles, too.

Seafood and meats are marinated and fried crisp in coconut oil before they are pickled in vinegar and spices. Coconut vinegar is preferred, but any other vinegar can be substituted. Sesame oil is usually used to season the pickling spices, but any vegetable oil can be used instead. A pickle must be kept for at least a week before eating, allowing the principal ingredient to mellow and absorb spices.

Salted Mango Pickle

Uppu Manga Achaar

Small tender green mangoes or larger raw green mangoes can be used for this pickle. The raw green mangoes should be kept in hay for two days to make them soft and tart. Large salted mangoes can be used for curries and chutneys. The tender salted mangoes are used to make tender mango pickle which is then chopped and mixed with onions and green chillis for a spicy accompaniment.

12 cups water
3 cups coarse sea salt
½ teaspoon ground turmeric
2 pounds whole green mangoes, washed and
    patted dry

In a large pot, bring the water with the salt to a boil. When it is boiling, remove from the heat and cool.

Add the turmeric to the cooled water and stir. Put the mangoes in a large sterilized ceramic or glass jar, and pour in the salt solution until the mangoes are completely immersed. Screw the jar tightly shut, so that it is completely airtight, and store in a cool place.

The pickle will be ready in a month. The large green mangoes will be soft by then, and the tender mangoes will be hard and wrinkled.

Tender Mango Pickle

Kanni Manga Achaar

Small tender green mangoes are used to make this simply prepared pickle traditionally stored in a barani (ceramic pickling jar). The pickled mangoes are served sliced with sliced shallots, green chillis, and a spoonful of warm coconut oil drizzled over.

1 pound small tender green mangoes
1 cup salt
½ cup chilli powder, lightly roasted
½ cup mustard powder
1 teaspoon asafoetida
1 teaspoon ground fenugreek
¼ cup sesame seed oil

Mix the mangoes with the salt in a glass or ceramic bowl and set aside for a day.

Add the remaining ingredients to the mangoes.

Store in an airtight sterilized glass or ceramic jar for a month, shaking the jar occasionally to stir the contents.

Mustard and Mango Pickle

Kaduku Manga Achaar

The coarse husked mustard enhances the flavor of the tart green mangoes. This pickle is usually stored for a month until the spices and mango pieces have blended and matured, but it can also be freshly prepared and served immediately with chopped shallots.

4 cups diced unpeeled green mangoes
½ cup salt
½ cup water
½ cup sesame oil
6 cloves garlic, sliced
1 tablespoon sliced fresh ginger
8 curry leaves
5 tablespoons chilli powder
½ teaspoon ground turmeric
½ cup mustard powder
½ cup vinegar

Mix the mango pieces with 2 teaspoons of the salt in a ceramic or glass bowl and set aside for a day. Then remove the mango pieces from the salty liquid and discard the liquid.

Mix the water with the rest of the salt in a small pot and bring to a boil; strain and set aside.

Heat the oil in a medium pot, add the garlic, ginger, and curry leaves and sauté for 2 minutes. Add the chilli powder, turmeric, and mustard powder, and sauté over low heat for 1 minute. Add the vinegar, salt solution, and mango pieces, and cook for a few minutes.

Allow mixture to cool and then store in a sterilized bottle.

Sun-dried Mango Pickle

Ada Manga Achaar

Strips of green mango are salted and left to dry in the sun on woven mats for up to 2 weeks, until they are soft and slightly leathery. This method is what gives this pickle its distinctive taste.

Mix the mangoes with the sea salt and set aside in an earthenware pot for a day.

The next day, spread the mango pieces out on a woven mat set outside in the sun. Dry the mangoes in the sun for 2 weeks, or until they are soft and dry.

Heat the sesame oil in a heavy skillet and fry the ginger, garlic, and curry leaves for 2 minutes. Lower the heat and add the chilli powder, turmeric, and asafoetida, stirring until slightly heated. Add the dried mango slices and cane sugar, and stir until this mixture has coated the mangoes. Taste and add more salt if necessary.

Remove the mango mixture from the heat and cool completely before storing in a sterilized glass or ceramic jar.

2 pounds raw green mangoes, peeled and sliced
   into thin strips
2 tablespoons coarse sea salt
½ cup sesame oil
1-inch piece fresh ginger, cut into strips
6 cloves garlic, thinly sliced
12 curry leaves
¼ cup chilli powder
1 teaspoon ground turmeric
1 teaspoon asafoetida
¼ cup raw cane sugar

Spicy Lime Pickle

Naranga Achaar

Spicy lime pickle with its many variations is a staple in every pickle cupboard in Kerala. This is a basic lime pickle with oil and spices which can be eaten with any meal. It is especially good with, and perfectly complements, Kanji (page 36).

24 limes, quartered
½ cup salt
¼ cup sesame oil
1 teaspoon mustard seeds
1 teaspoon fenugreek seeds
1 teaspoon sliced fresh ginger
12 cloves garlic, sliced
6 green chillis, slit
12 curry leaves
6 tablespoons chilli powder
1 teaspoon ground turmeric
1 teaspoon ground asafoetida
½ cup vinegar

TEN DAYS AHEAD:

Mix the limes with the salt in a ceramic bowl and store at room temperature for 10 days, stirring occasionally.

AFTER TEN DAYS:

Heat the sesame oil in a deep skillet. Add the mustard seeds and when they burst, lower the heat. Add the fenugreek seeds, ginger, garlic, green chillis, and curry leaves. Fry for 2 minutes, then add the chilli powder, turmeric, and asafoetida. Allow the spices to heat through slightly, then add the salted limes and vinegar. Taste and add more salt if necessary, and cook for 1 to 2 minutes, until the mixture starts boiling.

Remove lime mixture from the heat and cool completely before storing in sterilized glass jars.

Lime and Green Pepper Pickle

Narangayum Pacha Kurumolagu Achaar

Crisp green pepper berries are pickled with whole limes and a few select spices in this variation of lime pickle. Ask your local Indian store for green pepper berries on the stalk to savor the pungent crunch of fresh berries. Cut the limes open just before serving, and spoon the pickle juices and green pepper over the pieces of lime.

24 limes
½ cup salt
¼ cup oil
12 green chillis, slit
1 teaspoon sliced fresh ginger
8 cloves garlic, sliced
12 curry leaves
1 teaspoon ground turmeric
1 cup green pepper berries
½ cup lime juice

ONE WEEK AHEAD:

Mix the whole limes with the salt in a ceramic bowl and store for a week at room temperature, tossing occasionally.

AFTER A WEEK:

Heat the oil in a deep pot, and add the green chillis, ginger, garlic, and curry leaves. Fry for 2 minutes over medium heat, then add the turmeric and green pepper berries and cook for a few minutes, coating the berries with the seasoned oil. Add the salted limes and the lime juice, and remove from the heat.

Cool and store in sterilized jars. Keep for at least a week before using.

Lime and Raisin Pickle

Narangayum Mundiringa Achaar

This delicious pickle is sweet with puréed raisins and jaggery. It should be kept for a month or even longer before using, as the juices from the limes mellow and blend with the spices and raisin paste into a dark gelatinous pulp.

24 limes
½ cup salt
½ cup oil
12 curry leaves
1 teaspoon fenugreek seeds
6 tablespoons garlic paste
2 teaspoons ginger paste
1 tablespoon mustard powder
¼ cup chilli powder
1 teaspoon ground turmeric
1 teaspoon asafoetida
½ cup jaggery or dark brown sugar
1 cup raisins, ground to a paste

TEN DAYS AHEAD:

Mix the limes with the salt in a ceramic bowl and store for 10 days at room temperature, tossing occasionally.

AFTER 10 DAYS:

Heat the oil in a deep vessel and fry the curry leaves for 1 minute. Add the fenugreek seeds, garlic paste, and ginger paste and fry until the oil rises to the top.

Add the mustard powder, chilli powder, turmeric, and asafoetida, and continue frying for 2 more minutes.

Add the jaggery, ground raisins, and salted limes. Cook for 5 minutes or until the mixture is thick and the limes are well-coated with the spices.

Allow the lime mixture to cool and then store in sterilized jars for at least one month.

The Pickle Cupboard

In Kerala and other parts of India, a bottle of choice pickle is often gifted to the host, with the same panache as one would gift a special wine of rare vintage. The gift of a pickle is always appreciated and mothers, grandmothers, and aunts keep the younger generation in pickles until the young homemaker is prepared to venture into pickle-making herself.

At home, my collection of pickles are jealously hoarded in a cupboard kept just for pickles. On my last count, it had over twenty-five pickles, most given to me as gifts. Along with my own homemade pickles, I have an impressive array of favorites from all parts of the country— pickled bamboo shoot from Sikkim in the North East frontier; whole chillis stuffed with spices from Rajasthan; mango in mustard oil from Bengal; and pickled tamarind from Tamil Nadu. Also in the cupboard are cousin Reenie's chicken pickle brought on her visit to Kodaikanal; my sister-in-law Lata's *avakkai*, the mango fresh from her garden in Hyderabad; and my husband's cousin Mariamma's *loev loevi* pickle. Each holds a memory of a time or an event long past, and as the pickle is eaten, we reminisce and relive the moment.

In the corner, like an aged vintage wine, is a smoked gooseberry pickle that I surprised my family with recently, given to me by an aunt, deceased over a decade ago. An early '95 vintage *nellika karapichathu*!

Smoked Gooseberry Preserve

Nellikka Karapichathu

This is an old recipe for preserved gooseberries that keeps for years, as it has in my own pickle cupboard. Karinellikka, the Indian gooseberry, has a high content of vitamin C and is used in many ayurvedic medicines and supplements. Smoked and preserved in this way, it does not lose any of its valuable nutrients. Traditionally smoked in the glowing embers of a wood fire hearth, gooseberries can also be smoked in a modern kitchen. It will be ready for use within 2 months and can be pickled with spices, ground into a chutney with coconut, or sliced and served with chopped shallots.

2 pounds Indian gooseberries
½ pound sea salt
¼ pound kandhari or whole green chillis

Place the gooseberries with the salt and green chillis in a deep earthen clay pot or any other pot. Pour in enough water to immerse the gooseberries and cover with a thin muslin cloth. Bring to a boil and then lower the heat and simmer for 10 minutes. Remove from the heat and cool.

Put a small container with smoking coals into the pot of gooseberries. Cover and simmer over low heat for 20 minutes. Remove the coals and shake the pot around gently to stir its contents. Repeat this step daily for a week, until the liquid evaporates and the gooseberries darken and shrivel.

After a week, the preserve can be stored in a sterilized ceramic jar. Keep in a cool place for at least 2 months before using.

Bitter Gourd Pickle

Pavakka Achaar

This is a mildly spiced pickle for bitter gourd lovers that can be used immediately.

Mix 1 teaspoon of the salt and the bitter gourd slices in a ceramic bowl and set aside for 3 hours to draw out the bitterness. Then drain and squeeze out the water that collects and spread the bitter gourd on a tray to dry for an hour.

Heat the oil in a skillet and add the mustard seeds. When they burst, add the ginger, garlic, green chillis, and curry leaves, and fry for 1 minute.

Add the bitter gourd slices and fry for 1 minute.

Add the vinegar, remaining teaspoon of salt, and turmeric, and cook for 5 minutes, until the bitter gourd is soft. Cool and store in sterilized jars.

2 teaspoons salt
12 bitter gourds, sliced into thin semicircles
1 tablespoon oil
1 teaspoon mustard seeds
1 teaspoon slivered fresh ginger
6 cloves garlic, sliced
3 green chillis, slit
6 curry leaves
1 cup vinegar
½ teaspoon ground turmeric

Brinjal Pickle
Vazhadhananga Achaar

This is my mother's recipe for sweet-and-sour eggplant pickle. This pickle does not keep for long, so keep it refrigerated in warm weather. Try this pickle in a sandwich or chop fine to make a spicy dip.

½ pound eggplant, cut into ½-inch wedges
1 tablespoon salt
½ cup sesame oil
1 teaspoon minced fresh ginger
8 cloves garlic, sliced
2 green chillis, slit
1 teaspoon fenugreek seeds
2 tablespoons mustard seeds, ground to a paste
  with a little vinegar
1 tablespoon chilli powder
½ teaspoon ground turmeric
1 teaspoon finely ground black pepper
1 teaspoon ground cumin
1 cup vinegar
2 tablespoons sugar

Mix the eggplant with the salt and set aside in a colander for an hour. Wipe the eggplant dry with a paper towel.

Heat the sesame oil in a deep skillet and fry the eggplant in two batches until light brown. Remove the eggplant when browned and set aside.

In the same skillet, add the ginger, garlic, green chillis, and fenugreek seeds and fry for 1 minute. Add the mustard paste and fry until the oil rises to the top.

Add the chilli powder, turmeric, pepper, and cumin and fry, stirring continuously, until the oil rises to the top once again.

Add the vinegar, sugar, fried eggplant, and more salt if needed, and simmer for 5 minutes or until the pickle is thick.

Remove from the heat, cool, and store in sterilized bottles in the refrigerator.

Fish Pickle
Meen Achaar

There are two ways to make a fish pickle—in a thin vinegar and spice mix, or with a thick spice mix that is almost a curry. This recipe is for the first type of pickle; if you prefer a thicker pickle base, use the recipe for beef pickle (page 205). You can also use this recipe for shrimp and other seafood pickles.

Mix the fish pieces with half the salt and all the turmeric in a ceramic bowl and set aside for an hour.

Heat the coconut oil in a skillet, add the fish and fry for 2 minutes or until lightly browned. Remove from the oil and set aside.

Add the sesame oil to the used coconut oil. Add the ginger, garlic, green chillis, and fenugreek seeds and fry for 1 minute.

Add the chilli powder and pepper and fry, stirring continuously, until the oil rises to the top.

Add the fried fish pieces, vinegar, and the rest of the salt, and simmer for 2 minutes. Remove from the heat, cool, and store the fish pickle in sterilized bottles.

1 pound filleted fish, cut into 1-inch cubes
1 tablespoon salt
½ teaspoon ground turmeric
¼ cup coconut oil
¼ cup sesame oil
1 teaspoon slivered fresh ginger
6 cloves garlic, sliced
3 green chillis, slit
1 teaspoon fenugreek seeds
2 teaspoons chilli powder
½ teaspoon finely ground black pepper
1½ cups vinegar

Minced Shrimp Pickle

Chemmeen Kothu Achaar

This is a sweet-and-sour pickle with minced shrimps in a vinegar and mustard base—great as a sandwich filling.

Mix the minced shrimp with the salt in a ceramic bowl and set aside for an hour.

Heat the sesame oil in a deep skillet and fry the shrimp for 2 minutes or until lightly browned. Remove from the oil and set aside.

Add the sliced shallots to the same skillet and fry for 1 to 2 minutes, until they are soft and transparent. Add the ginger, garlic, green chillis, and fenugreek and fry for 1 minute. Add the mustard paste and fry until the oil rises to the top.

Add the chili powder, cumin, turmeric, and fry, stirring continuously, until the oil again rises to the top. Add the vinegar, sugar, shrimp, and more salt if needed. Simmer for 5 minutes, until the pickle is thick.

Remove shrimp pickle from the heat, cool, and store in sterilized bottles.

½ pound shrimp, peeled, cooked, and coarsely minced
1 tablespoon salt
½ cup sesame oil
24 shallots, thinly sliced
1 teaspoon minced fresh ginger
12 cloves garlic, sliced
3 green chillis, slit
1 teaspoon ground fenugreek
2 teaspoons mustard seeds, ground to a paste with a little vinegar
2 teaspoons chilli powder
1 teaspoon ground cumin
½ teaspoon ground turmeric
1 cup vinegar
1 tablespoon sugar

Mussel Pickle

Kallumekka Achaar

This is a spicy pickle from the Malabar region, famous for the variety of its shellfish.

Mix the mussels with 1 teaspoon of the salt, 1 teaspoon of the chilli powder, and ½ teaspoon of the turmeric. Set aside for an hour.

Heat the coconut oil in a wok and fry the mussels for 4 to 5 minutes, until brown and crisp. Remove the mussels and set aside.

Add the sesame oil to the used coconut oil and heat. Add the ginger, garlic, and curry leaves and fry for 1 minute. Add the fenugreek and mustard paste, then add the remaining chilli powder and turmeric, and continue to fry until the oil rises to the top.

Add the mussels and fry for a few minutes, until the mussels are coated with the spices.

Add the vinegar and remaining teaspoon of salt, and cook until the pickle has thickened. Remove from the heat, cool, and store in a sterilized glass jar.

2 cups mussels, cleaned, bearded, and shelled
2 teaspoons salt
3 tablespoons chilli powder
1 teaspoon ground turmeric
¼ cup coconut oil
¾ cup sesame oil
1 tablespoon sliced fresh ginger
1 tablespoon sliced fresh garlic
8 curry leaves
1 teaspoon ground fenugreek
1 tablespoon mustard seeds, ground to a paste with a little vinegar
½ cup vinegar

Beef Pickle
Moori Erachi Achaar

This pickle has a thick, delicious gravy. The recipe was given to me by Jessie, a friend in Kodaikanal, whose gentle persuasion prompted me to venture into pickle-making. Fish, shrimp, pork, chicken, or any other meat can also be pickled using this recipe. My sister Latha even used it to make a meatball pickle.

1 pound stewing beef, cut into ½-inch cubes
1 tablespoon salt
3 cups water
1 cup vinegar
¼ cup coconut oil
½ cup sesame oil
1 teaspoon ginger paste
2 tablespoons garlic paste
3 green chillis, slit
6 curry leaves
1 teaspoon fenugreek seeds
2 teaspoons mustard seeds, ground to a paste
    with a little vinegar
2 teaspoons chilli powder
½ teaspoon ground turmeric
2 tablespoons ground coriander
1 teaspoon finely ground black pepper

In a medium pot, cook the beef with the salt, water, and ¼ cup of the vinegar until tender and the water has evaporated.

Heat the coconut oil in a skillet, add the beef and fry until lightly browned. Remove from the oil and set aside.

Add the sesame oil to the coconut oil and heat. Add the ginger and garlic pastes, green chillis, curry leaves, and fenugreek seeds and fry for 2 minutes. Add the mustard paste and fry until the oil rises to the top.

Add the chilli powder, turmeric, coriander, and pepper and fry, stirring continuously, until the oil again rises to the top.

Add the beef, remaining ¾ cup of vinegar, and more salt if needed. Simmer for 3 to 5 minutes, until the pickle is thick.

Remove from the heat, cool, and store in sterilized bottles.

Traveling Chefs, Bormas, and How to Cook for a Hundred Guests

In earlier times, weddings, engagement ceremonies, and christenings in large Syrian Christian families required the services of the traveling chef. Most clans had family favorites, and the virtues of Andhoni's lace-rimmed *paalappams* or Cook Varghese's pork roast were remembered long after the occasions that featured them.

The cook arrived days before the event and did the planning with the family. The meals and menus, the marketing, the helpers required, the firewood, the vessels, the best fish, and the many details that go into the success of a well-conducted function were discussed and sorted out. The Syrian Christian housewife, known for her proficiency in cooking and house-keeping, kept a record of all expenditures. The *nadathukaran* (literally the "man who makes it happen"), usually the farm or estate manager, helped with the budgeting and planning.

The main meal itself, though hardly lavish, featured a variety of traditional Syrian Christian fare, prepared for days. The *Meen Vevichathu* was prepared first, and reheated daily over a low flame with a deft shake, the sour red gravy growing darker and thicker. *Erachi Olathiathu*, stir-fried beef with tender coconut chips, was prepared next, and sautéed until the meat was dark brown and crisp with the coating of spices. Pickles and *vepilakatti* (curry leaf powder), prepared months earlier, were inspected for spoilage. *Palahaarams* of all kinds, made for several weeks prior, were brought out of the storeroom, and this was where the housewife showed her versatility. *Kachiya Moru*, vegetable *thorans*, stew, and *appams* were made on the day of the function, along with the cook's specials—thin slices of spicy pork roast or duck roast with potatoes and onions. A funeral breakfast or a tea following a seventh-day mass, however, may feature just *appams* and stew, and a variety of *palahaarams*.

Mrs. B. F. Varghese, whose cookbook has traveled to distant shores with many a new homemaker, this author included, has a chapter titled, "When You Cook for a Hundred Guests," in which traditional Syrian Christian favorites that are standard fare at all functions are outlined in recipes sufficient for large gatherings. In this book she dispenses all sorts of valuable advice, such as, "If you make large quantities of cutlets, it is easier to roll them thickly on a floured board and cut with sandwich cutters or tumblers."

Festive occasions in large estate houses were celebrated until very recently in much the same way, with the addition of a baked vegetable au gratin à la chef Andhoni, or large trays of chocolate mousse concocted by a talented cousin. By the 1980s, most functions were catered by private caterers, but soon the ubiquitous *biryani* edged out such feasts. (A meal in one, *biryani* has spiced meat cooked into a *kurma*, and simmered with rice, and is served with a yogurt salad and a date chutney.) By the year 2000, the trend changed again, and most celebrations are now held at the five-star hotels that have sprung up all over Kerala.

Early on, there were also chefs who traveled to homes in distant estates and townships to teach the womenfolk the fine art of baking and Western cooking. This marked the introduction of desserts, puddings, cakes, and biscuits (cookies). Pachheek was a master chef of Portuguese origin who traveled to many Syrian Christian homes for a day of baking and cooking lessons. Several such households, newly accustomed to the joys of freshly baked bread and cakes, installed *bormas* in their homes—wood-fired brick ovens with a large roomy interior in which bread, cakes, and butter biscuits were baked. Pachheek would arrive with a helper, and a flurry of activity would follow. Impromptu baking pans were ingeniously fashioned out of old biscuit tins, and hours later the kitchen tables were groaning with baked goods that would be stored in large tins in the storeroom. Commercially run bakeries made an appearance soon after, and today, every self-respecting town and village in Kerala boasts of a Best Bakery.

My mother's story of a female chef who made the rounds of prominent Syrian Christian homes in the 1940s had us enthralled. Missy, as she was known, was an Anglo-Indian, and her speciality was Western dishes, of which the Syrian Christian housewife had little knowledge. Anxious to master the art of baking and roasting, the community welcomed her into their homes where she conducted cooking classes for the women of the family. Cakes and puddings, roasts, baked vegetable dishes in béchamel sauce, breaded chops, and stuffed cutlets were some of the recipes in her repertoire of Anglo-Indian dishes. A devout Christian, she would stay at a local convent, where she was given a room in exchange for the cooking classes she held for the sisters in her spare time.

One evening, as the story goes, a young nun grew worried since Missy had not opened the door in spite of her persistent knocking. Peeping through the keyhole, she spied Missy hurriedly pulling a dress over her head, turning just then to reveal she was actually a man!

Tender coconut being scooped out of its shell

PUDDINGS AND PAYASAMS

Malayalis rarely prepare special sweets or puddings to eat as dessert after a meal. Instead, they dip into the stock of sweets from the storeroom—sticky slices of halvahs, syrupy *churuttu*, or crisp *cheedas*. Fresh yogurt and *paani* is also a favorite, with a banana sliced in. In country homes, a lump of brown *sarkara* (unrefined cane sugar) suffices to sweeten the palate after a spicy meal. And there are always the fruits of the season—fresh pineapple, mangoes, bananas, jackfruit, mangosteen, rambutans, guavas, and papayas.

For the special occasion, however, *payasam*—a sweet porridge with milk or coconut milk sweetened with sugar or jaggery—is prepared. *Payasams* can be made from a range of vegetables and fruits, from sweet whole mangoes to mung beans. I was puzzled when I was served a delicious *payasam* at a party; the flavor was familiar but could it be? I was surprised when I was told the mystery ingredient was exactly what I had suspected—finely shredded cabbage!

More recently, with the advent of western influences, soufflés and puddings are prepared in the Syrian Christian kitchen using such fresh local produce as mango, pineapple, and tender coconut. With the increased availability of western ingredients such as cocoa, vanilla (both now grown in Kerala), and gelatin, it is not uncommon to find a perfectly turned out chocolate mousse or Black Forest cake at an estate bungalow wedding in the middle of nowhere!

Payasam—Food for the Gods

This sublime combination of milk and sugar, called *kheer* in Northern India and *payasam* in Southern India, is arguably one of the oldest desserts in the world. References to this dish can be found in ancient Indian scriptures, folklore, and legends. Crossing religious and cultural barriers, *payasam* is a universal offering to the gods in temples, churches, and even mosques all over India.

The legendary dried fruit *kheer* made at the tomb of a famous Sufi saint in Ajmer in Rajasthan attracts pilgrims from around the country. As the massive cauldron is drained rapidly, pilgrims are even known to jump in to scrape the remains of the blessed *tabarruk* from the bottom. At St. Antony's church in Kochi in Kerala, parishioners queue up anually for the famous *kadum payasam* which keeps for a whole year—till the next festival.

Kerala's most well-known *payasam* is made in the Sri Krishna temple in Ambalapuzha. As legend has it, the king of this region was defeated in a game of chess by Lord Krishna who was disguised as a sage, and was cleverly outwitted into promising what amounted to a billion tons of rice. All the rice in the land and in the kingdoms nearby would not suffice, so the king promised to pay this over time as *payasam* to the pilgrims at the temple—and so it continues to this day.

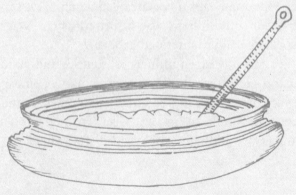

Steamed Rice Paste Porridge

Adaprathaman

This is the classic payasam *of Kerala, made with previously prepared or storebought* ada *(steamed rice paste flakes), cooked with raw cane sugar and coconut milk, and delicately flavored with ginger and cardamom. If store-bought* ada *is used, it is essential to first sauté the dried rice flakes in ghee or butter to keep them from sticking together. When* ada *was unavailable in Bombay, my mother would make this* payasam *with chopped leftover* chapatis *(a whole-wheat flatbread), which gave it a wholesome smoky flavor.*

Heat the ghee in a deep skillet and add the store-bought rice flakes and sauté them for a few minutes.

Add the thin coconut milk, jaggery, cardamom, and ginger and simmer for 8 to 10 minutes over low heat, until the rice flakes are cooked and soft.

Add the thick coconut milk and simmer for 2 more minutes, until the *payasam* is thick and creamy.

Serves 4

1 tablespoon ghee or butter
1 cup steamed rice paste flakes, store-bought or homemade (*see below*)
2 cups thin coconut milk
¼ cup jaggery or dark brown sugar
½ teaspoon cardamom powder
¼ teaspoon ground ginger
½ cup thick coconut milk

Steamed Rice Paste Flakes   Ada

Prepare a steamer with water in its base.

Cut the banana leaves into 5-inch squares. Wilt the leaves over a flame, so they are easy to roll, and then grease with the ghee.

In a small bowl, mix the rice flour with just enough water to make a thick paste, like pancake batter.

Spread enough batter on each leaf to cover with a thin layer. Roll up each leaf and place in the steamer.

Cook for 8 to 10 minutes, then open the leaves carefully, and cut the steamed dough into ½-inch squares. Use fresh in this recipe; do not sauté in ghee as with store-bought *ada*.

2 large banana leaves
1 tablespoon ghee, melted
1 cup rice flour, sifted
Water, as needed

Vermicelli Porridge

Semiya Payasam

This is a quickly prepared sweet porridge made with fine vermicelli. The ghee that is used to prepare all Indian sweets can be replaced by butter. You can also replace the vermicelli with a cup of toasted semolina for rava payasam—semolina porridge.

Slightly heat the ghee over low heat in a large pot and fry the cashews. As they turn golden brown, add the raisins. When the raisins puff up, add the vermicelli and cardamom. Stir-fry until light brown in color.

Add the water, milk, and sugar, and cook for 2 to 3 minutes, until the payasam is thick and creamy.

Serves 4

1 tablespoon ghee or butter
6 fresh cashews
¼ cup raisins
1 cup vermicelli
¼ teaspoon ground cardamom
2 cups water
4 cups milk
½ cup sugar

Ripe Mango Porridge

Pazhamanga Payasam

This payasam is best made with the tiny chakkara manga (sugar mangoes) that ripen in the heat of summer. Serve hot or cold.

Steam the whole mangoes until they are soft, then remove the skin.

Put the thin coconut milk and sugar in a deep pot and bring to just below a boil. Add the skinned mangoes and cook for 8 minutes over low heat, until the coconut milk has cooked down to 2 cups.

Add the thick coconut milk and heat through. Sprinkle with cinnamon just before serving.

Serves 4

4 small ripe mangoes
6 cups thin coconut milk
1 cup sugar
1 cup thick coconut milk
½ teaspoon ground cinnamon

VARIATIONS: This recipe can also be used to make Plantain Porridge or Jackfruit Porridge; follow the recipe, but substitute chopped plantains or jackfruit for the mangoes and use cardamom instead of cinnamon to enhance the distinct flavors of those fruits.

Rice Porridge

Paal Payasam

This is a simply prepared porridge of milk and rice similar to rice pudding, flavored with cardamom and caramelized sugar. The legendary Ambalapuzha Paal Payasam *prepared in the temple is often ordered in large amounts for weddings and functions.* Paal Payasam *is also deliciously wholesome when made with broken red country rice instead of white rice. This payasam is best served cold and can be kept refrigerated for days.*

Drain the rice and place in a medium pot with the 2 cups of water. Cook for 4 to 5 minutes, until the water has been absorbed. Transfer the rice to a wide, shallow pot or casserole with a heavy bottom.

Add the milk, sugar, cardamom seeds, and caramel syrup to the rice and stir to combine. Cook over low heat, stirring occasionally, for 12 to 15 minutes, until the rice is soft and the porridge thick and creamy.

Heat the ghee in a small skillet and fry the cashews until golden brown. Add the raisins and when they swell, pour the garnish mixture over the *payasam*.

NOTE: To make the caramel syrup, heat 2 tablespoons of sugar in a small pan over low heat until it melts and becomes golden brown.

Serves 4

1 cup white rice, soaked in water for 2 hours
2 cups water
12 cups milk
2 cups sugar
1 teaspoon ground cardamom seeds
2 tablespoons caramel syrup (see Note)
1 tablespoon ghee or butter, for garnish
4 fresh cashews, halved, for garnish
12 raisins, for garnish

Mung Bean Porridge

Cherupayaru Payasam

Another classic payasam *from Kerala, this is a wholesome porridge of split mung beans and coconut milk sweetened with raw cane sugar. This is a hearty winter dessert when served hot but it can also be served cold.*

Toast the mung beans in a deep skillet, stirring continuously for 2 minutes so they lose their rawness. Add the water, thin coconut milk, and ginger, and simmer for 15 to 20 minutes, until the beans are soft.

Add the jaggery and cardamom and cook for 5 minutes over low heat, mashing the mixture if needed till it becomes slightly mushy. Now add the thick coconut milk and cook for 5 more minutes over low heat, until the porridge is soft and creamy.

Heat the ghee in a small skillet, add the coconut pieces and fry for 2 minutes or until they are a golden brown. Add the raisins and when they swell, pour the garnish over the *payasam*.

Serves 4

2 cups split mung beans
6 cups water
4 cups thin coconut milk
½ teaspoon ground ginger
1 cup jaggery or dark brown sugar
1 teaspoon ground cardamom
1 cup thick coconut milk
1 teaspoon ghee or butter, for garnish
¼ cup thinly sliced fresh coconut, for garnish
12 raisins, for garnish

Coconut Milk and Molasses Pudding

Thenga Paalum Sarkara Pudding

This creamy baked pudding has a delicious blend of flavors—coconut milk, jaggery, and nutmeg. *Serve hot or cold.*

Serves 6

Preheat the oven to a moderate temperature (350 degrees F). Grease a 9 x 13-inch baking dish.

In a saucepan heat the sugar for 1 to 2 minutes, until it caramelizes to a golden brown. Pour into the prepared baking dish.

In a bowl, mix well the milk, coconut milk, condensed milk, and eggs. Stir in the jaggery or brown sugar. Strain into the baking dish over the caramel.

Sprinkle the nutmeg over the pudding. Place the baking dish in a tray of water to a depth halfway up the side of the baking dish, and bake until the pudding is firm.

2 tablespoons sugar
4 cups milk
2 cups thick coconut milk
½ cup thickened or condensed milk
4 eggs, well beaten
1 cup jaggery or brown sugar
1 teaspoon grated nutmeg

Tender Coconut Pudding

Karikku Pudding

This delicately flavored dessert is the perfect end to a spicy meal. The agar (available at Asian groceries) can be replaced by gelatin. For a delicious ice cream, replace the agar or gelatin with a cup of heavy cream and churn in an ice-cream maker.

Serves 6

2 large, very tender coconuts, flesh scooped out
    and coconut water reserved
1 can condensed milk
3 sheets agar or 2 (½-ounce) envelopes
    unflavored gelatin
½ cup warm milk

Purée half of the coconut pieces with 1 cup of coconut water in a blender. Chop the remaining coconut and stir into the mixture along with the remaining coconut water and the condensed milk. Set aside.

Soak the agar or gelatin in the warm milk until completely dissolved. Add to the coconut mixture and stir well. (NOTE: If using agar, strain the milk into the coconut mixture.)

Pour the pudding into a large dish or individual bowls and leave to set in the refrigerator for 2 hours. Serve sprinkled with a few fresh rose petals and/or honey.

Coconut Pancakes
Madakappams

*This is a delicately flavored dessert pancake with the charac-
teristic Malayali flavors of coconut and cardamom. These
pancakes are made with white flour—ironically called
'American mavu' (mavu meaning flour) in Kerala, as the
first supplies of pure white wheat flour came from the United
States and the name stuck. Serve warm with coconut milk
and cane sugar sauce.*

PREPARE THE FILLING:

In a medium bowl, mix all the filling ingredients and
set aside.

PREPARE THE PANCAKE BATTER:

Mix the thin coconut milk with the beaten eggs and
add the salt. Stir in the sifted flour and make a thin,
runny batter without lumps, adding water as needed.

Grease a skillet with a little oil and heat until a
spoonful of batter sizzles when dropped into the pan.
Pour half a cup of batter into the skillet, swirling around
to form a thin pancake. Cover with a lid and cook for 1
minute until firm. Remove the pancake from the pan
and immediately place 2 tablespoons of the filling on
one side of the pancake. Roll up and keep warm as you
prepare the rest from the remaining batter and filling.

PREPARE THE SAUCE:

In a small pan, mix together the thick coconut milk
and cane sugar and heat until warm.

Serve the warm pancakes topped with the sauce.

Makes 8 to 10

PANCAKES:
2 cups thin coconut milk
2 eggs, beaten
¼ teaspoon salt
2 cups white flour, sifted
Water, as needed
Oil for frying

FILLING:
2 cups grated fresh coconut
¼ cup sugar
½ teaspoon ground cardamom

SAUCE:
1 cup thick coconut milk
½ cup raw cane sugar

Caramelized Plantains with Coconut Cream

Nendrikkai *(large cooking plantains) are browned in caramel in this delightful recipe, then simmered in a coconut milk sauce. Serve hot, sprinkled with cinnamon.*

Heat the sugar in a heavy skillet for 1 minute until it melts but does not change color. Add the lemon juice, and place the plantains in the sugar syrup. Cook slowly for 2 to 3 minutes, until the sugar caramelizes. Brown the plantains on both sides.

Add the coconut milk and cook covered over low heat for 5 minutes. Remove from heat when the plantains are tender and the coconut milk has thickened to a creamy sauce. Sprinkle with cinnamon and serve.

Serves 4

¼ cup sugar
1 teaspoon lemon juice
4 ripe plantains, peeled
2 cups thick coconut milk
1 teaspoon ground cinnamon

Mango Mousse

This creamy fruit mousse can be set in individual bowls or in a large serving bowl. It can also be prepared with other puréed tropical fruit, such as jackfruit, guava, pineapple, avocado or passion fruit. Like Tender Coconut Pudding (page 216), it makes a delicious ice cream. Garnish with cream and fresh sliced mango.

In a large mixing bowl, lightly blend the mango purée, yogurt, cream, and sugar syrup.

Fold in the chopped mango and pour into a serving dish. Sprinkle with cinnamon and leave to set in a refrigerator for 3 hours.

NOTE: To prepare sugar syrup, dissolve ½ cup sugar in ½ cup water and cook for 3 minutes over medium heat. Cool before using in the recipe.

Serves 6

4 cups fresh mango purée, plus 1 cup finely chopped mango
2 cups thick (Greek) yogurt
1 cup heavy cream
½ cup sugar syrup (*see Note*)
½ teaspoon ground cinnamon

A Sweet Ending

The Syrian Christian housewife is a perfectionist in every culinary venture she undertakes. In the early 1990s, when the fine art of icing elaborate cakes had taken the skilled housewives of the Syrian Christian community by storm, each tried to outdo the other. Women vied to produce the finest cake icing with the most realistic roses and the laciest lattice work. Once, the young daughters of a particular family were anxious to show off their latest sugary collections of exotic orchids with delicately tinted petals and leaves. Late that night, as they were working, tragedy struck. Their grandmother, who was to see their work the next day, unexpectedly passed away. Unfazed, they decided to take their beautiful creations to their grandmother. They arranged the beautiful iced flowers around her coffin to be admired by the entire community, knowing that their grandmother would have heartily approved.

Birdsong in Injathotti

This was a rare occasion. My husband, George, and his siblings usually met in Kodaikanal, but as we were all in Kerala for a family wedding, we planned to drive to their uncle's estate in Injathotti at the foothills of the Munnar High Ranges. Achen had asked for us. He had not seen us for a long time, he said with an urgency in his soft voice. He had to make some decisions about the future, and he wanted to do it now.

Achen and Ammai lived on their estate in Injathotti with Martin, the son they had adopted forty years earlier. Martin was mentally retarded, as Ammai would say. She was unaware of the political incorrectness of this word, and would probably retort, if informed, that fancy words would not change his condition. When they had discovered this, the nuns from the orphanage had offered to take him back and replace him with a healthy baby. But Ammai and Achen had refused. They had grown to love the nine-month-old baby they had waited so long for, and decided they would look after him as well as they could. Achen and Ammai, both gentle and sweet-natured, did a fine job; Martin grew up to be a cheerful young man who helped around the house occasionally, and needed to be helped in turn for certain things. He was mostly content, wandering around the estate singing the many hymns he loved in a strong baritone that belied his childlike demeanor.

At the Kothamangalam junction, we planned our route. We had been told that the road to Injathotti was not traversable after the heavy monsoons. After some discussion, it was decided that we would drive through a neighboring estate and then take the ferryboat across the Periyar, the big river, majestic and swollen even now, months after the monsoons.

Achen and Ammai were waiting on the verandah of their estate house, their gentle smiles welcoming us. Achen was my father-in-law's oldest brother, and we often remarked on how different the two siblings were even though they looked alike. Looking at them, any doubt of their Syrian ancestry was quickly dispelled. Fair-skinned with cropped, curly hair and large hooked noses, one could imagine them wearing a skull cap or a *distasha* and living somewhere in the Middle East.

Any similarities they had ended there though. My father-in-law, dynamic and charismatic, had left the small town they had grown up in and made his life in the hill stations of Ooty and Kodaikanal. Adopting Western ways, he dressed impeccably in well-tailored suits, polished boots, and berets. His older brother, content with rural life, had stayed on to cultivate his land and was never seen in anything but a spotless white *mundu* and shirt. Their wives were different from each other as well. My mother-in-law, tall, gray-eyed, and elegant, loved to attend the races in Bangalore and could hold her own in political discussions with the men. Ammai, on the other hand, dressed in simple cotton saris, her pleasant face lighting up frequently with a sweet smile. These differences didn't keep them apart and the two couples would often meet in each other's homes. This had ended with the death of my father-in-law followed months later by the death of my mother-in-law.

We were welcomed and led to the dining room, just off the large country kitchen, where a feast awaited us on the long wooden table—*Puttu, Erachi Olathiathu*, soft mounds of tapioca, an earthenware *chatti* of fiery *Meen Vevichathu*, thick slices of fruit cake and pineapple, hot plantain fritters, rosa cookies, and spiced *kozhalappam* rolls. Ammai fussed over us as we took our places, piling food on our plates and bringing out more tins of *palahaarams*, worrying that there was not enough. We savored the smoky, authentic flavor of simple country fare cooked the old way in a wood-fire hearth.

George teased Ammai about the way she fussed over us, saying she was treating us as if we were still the young children she used to feed in the past; indeed we did feel like children again, as Achen and Ammai tempted us with our favorite foods.

Later when we were seated in the living room, we noticed the stoop in Ammai's strong, capable shoulders and the vagueness in Achen's smile. They had aged considerably since we had seen them a year earlier. Ammai spoke then—they were worried about Martin's future. Would the convent care for him after their time if they left him an inheritance? Martin stood nearby, laughing as he heard his name. He sang constantly, and now he hummed loudly, *hoshannah*… He disliked the popular songs, preferring instead the religious music he played endlessly on his little tape recorder.

Achen said nothing, but nodded as Ammai spoke. They had to make decisions about the future. Relatives had been pressing them to sell the house and estate, too large for them to manage now. Perhaps they should move to a smaller house in the city? Or maybe a relative could move in with them? Ammai had someone in mind, but what if that did not work out? Looking at the various options, we told her firmly that she must stay on in this house. This had been their home for many years, where Ammai grew obscenely large gloxemias in her bedroom verandah, while Achen experimented with vanilla vines and organic tapioca, and from where Martin walked over each morning to the chapel in the convent nearby, as he had done since he was a little boy.

Ammai was clearly relieved that we were telling her just what she wanted to hear and we realized that this strong, gentle woman had been carrying a heavy burden for far too long. Though there were workers around the estate and in the house, she still took care of Martin, who had the occasional accident, and watched over Achen, who had become vague and dreamy, nodding at everything with a smile. We talked for hours, offering various solutions and options, realizing however that Ammai was really on her own.

The next morning after breakfast, we walked around the garden where Ammai grew African violets, begonias, and crotons. She had pots of extra plants that she had thoughtfully planted for visitors who asked for them. The garden was alive with the raucous twittering of birds which congregated in large numbers this time of year. Ammai remarked that these birds woke them up early each morning with birdsong so unmusical, she wished the nuns from the convent nearby would teach them to sing.

Achen, who had not spoken much the previous night, was now more vocal. He took us around the estate where everything grew in glorious abundance. Here in the foothills of the High Ranges, the soil was rich and fertile, even more so in this blessed region of Kerala, 'God's Own Country.' The rubber trees were well cared for with neat rainguards tucked into the slashes made in their trunks. The healthy plantain and tapioca plants, vanilla vines, and fruit trees proved that this was indeed a well-run estate. A large rambutan tree near the kitchen was heavy with ripe fruit. We picked up some which had dropped to the ground and were delighted by the succulent flavor. Achen hesitantly told us that he used no pesticides in the garden and that the fruit was all the better for it. The experts on the agricultural programs he watched on television claimed this was a new method called 'organic farming,' but this, Achen said, was the way he had always done it.

We were now at the *thodu*, the broad creek that flowed through the estate. The water was gently lapping at our feet, reflecting sunlight back onto the trees. Hanging our towels and change of clothing on a nearby tree, we stepped into the cool, clear water and soon were swimming without a care in the world. The creek was shallow in some parts, tumbling over large boulders in a soft froth as it slipped into a deep pool, then widening and meandering along its way. Bamboo groves, dense shrubs, and creepers with tiny white flowers grew in profusion, and the air was delicately scented with jasmine. To add to the sublime beauty, a peahen strutted past on the bank while her mate fanned out his magnificent plumage in a slow dance.

Some divine landscape designer had fashioned this with a perfection that could never be replicated, I remarked, wondering how I could re-create this scene in my next garden project. We splashed and frolicked for hours as Achen stood nearby, smiling indulgently.

We had planned to leave after lunch but when we eventually left, the sun was setting in the distant hills of Munnar. The birds were singing unharmoniously in the trees, and the huge rambutan tree was alive with a loud hum. Ammai and Achen had packed *palahaarams* in neat parcels for each family—little packets of rosa cookies, jackfruit halvah, and frosted rice balls. We waved and promised to visit again, soon. On the walk back, we were in high spirits, and sang all the way to the ferry landing, and continuing on the boat.

Back in Kodaikanal the next night, George called his aunt and uncle to thank them for their hospitality. Ammai said they had had a scare that morning. Achen had disappeared and they had looked for him everywhere. Finally Thomas, the estate manager, had found him swimming by himself in the little stream and had gently led him back to the house. When Ammai had berated him for wandering off, he said, "How could I resist after seeing how much fun the children were having yesterday?"

GLOSSARY

Special Terms in English

agar seaweed extract, a vegetarian substitute for gelatin

ash gourd *benincasa hispida* a large oval ash-colored gourd

ayurveda ancient Indian holistic system of healing

basmati a variety of long-grain Indian rice

biryani festive dish of rice layered with curried mutton or chicken

bell metal a combination of metals used for manufacturing bells and cooking vessels, mainly comprising of bronze and a smaller part of copper

bitter gourd *momordica charantia* long bitter fruit known for its medicinal properties; native to the tropical regions

breadfruit *artocarpis altilis* large fleshy fruit similar to tapioca, native of tropical regions

chickpea *cicer arietinum* garbanzo beans

Cornish hen small breed of poultry that originated in Cornwall, England

cowpea *vigna unguiculata* a grain legume grown in the tropics

crustacean hard-shelled marine life which includes lobster, crab, and shrimp

dessicated dehydrated

Dutch oven thick walled metal cooking pot with tight-fitting lid

dry-roast (*v*) heat (i.e spices) in ungreased heavy vessel over low heat

earthenware baked clay vessels used for cooking

fillet (*n*) boneless slice of fish or meat

freshwater fish fish found in lakes and streams

ghee clarified butter

hand-pounded (*i.e. rice*) pounded in stone vessel with wooden paddles

jackfruit *artocarpus heterophyllus* large segmented tropical fruit with strong flavor and aroma

jaggery unprocessed cane sugar

mackerel small sea fish of the family *scrombidae*

Malaya country now called Malaysia

Malayalis people of Kerala

Malayalam language of Kerala

mangoes *mangifera indica* a tropical fruit

mangosteen *garcinia mangostana a* tropical fruit

masala combination of spices

peacock, peahen *pava cristatus* national bird of India; male has brilliant plumage while the female of this species has only a crest of muted colors

palm syrup syrup obtained after processing the sap of the palmyra palm

plantain *plantago* a large cooking banana

pomfret flat medium-size fish of the family *bramidae*

rambutan *nephelium lappaceum* a tropical fruit

sauté/sautéed/sautéing lightly fried in oil

seerfish large fish also known as Spanish mackerel of the family *scombridae*

snake gourd *trichosanthes anguina* long snake-like vegetable

stir-fry sauté while continually stirring

toddy fermented sap of the coconut tree

Special Terms in Malayalam

achinga payaru slender runner bean

adupu wood stove

appa chatti small cast-iron wok used for cooking rice
   pancakes

appam steamed or fried cake

avial a medley of cooked vegetables (see page 54)

avalos podi roasted rice powder (see page 168)

barani ceramic jar used for pickling and wine making

beedi thin non-filter Indian cigarette with tobacco
   wrapped in dried leaves

brahmi *bacopa monnieri* medicinal herb which is used
   as a memory enhancer

chakka segmented fruit

chamandhi chutney, a crushed or ground relish of
   herbs and spices

chambanga water apple, a small heart-shaped fruit
   also called love apple

cheeda fried dough ball (see page 167)

cheena chatti round-bottomed cooking vessel of
   Chinese origin

cheera spinach or other greens

chembu large vessel for boiling water or tapioca

chemmeen shrimp

chena corn

chillimbikka sour gherkin-like fruit

choru unnu lunch or other meal, literally meaning *eat rice*

erachi meat

ethakka plantain

inja fibrous soapy scrub

inri appam unleavened bread served on Holy Thursday, named after the abbreviation INRI on the
   cross of Christ

ishtew stew (see page 127)

kaachiyathu simmered

kaapi coffee

karri curry

kaalanji backwater salmon

kalam cooking pot

kallu fermented coconut sap

kallappams fermented toddy cakes

kallumekka clams

kallu shaap toddy shop

kanji rice gruel (see page 36)

kappa tapioca

karimeen pearl spot, a backwater fish

Kavanni finely spun cotton fabric used for sari or shawl

kezhangu potato or other root vegetable

konju lobster

koon mushroom

koorka coleus tuber

kopa ceramic bowl used for rice gruel, coffee, or tea

kozhalappam sweet or savory roll (see pages 165 and
   166)

kozhi hen or rooster

kozhikotta steamed rice dumpling

kumbilappams steamed jackfruit and rice dumplings
   (see page 188)

kuru seed

maavu kuzhachathu cooked dough

manga mango

mani puttu steamed riceball cake (see page 39)

mannu chatti earthenware

marikolandu (*Tamil*) herb used in Tamil Nadu in
   South India to prevent nightmares

meen fish

meen chatti earthen pot in which fish is cooked

meen mutta fish roe

meen vevichathu curried fish

molee fish stewed with coconut milk (see page 90)

moringa oleifera (*Latin*) drumstick bean

moru spiced buttermilk

muraya koenigi (*Latin*) curry leaf

muringakka drumstick bean

nellu ara granary

neyappam molasses cake fried in clarified butter (see
   pages 186–187)

neyu ghee or clarified butter

olan vegetable dish made of red beans and pumpkin

olathiathu sautéed or stir-fried

onakka meen dried fish

orapera out-building set off the main kitchen for large-scale preparation of food

paalappam lace-rimmed pancake (see pages 40 and 41)

paani palmyra palm syrup

pachadi vegetable or fruit dish prepared with yogurt and coconut (see page 66)

palahaaram sweet or savory snack

palayamkodan a small tart banana

pappadam flatbread made with spiced lentil flour

parippu lentil

parotta a flat bread (see page 154)

pathiri a flat bread made with rice flour (see page 36)

pattichathu cooked down

payar bean

payasam sweet porridge

peralen thick spicy curry

pidi fistful

podi meen tiny fish

pollichathu method of cooking fish

ponni a short-grained polished rice used in South India

poovan small variety of banana

purattiathu mashed

puttu steamed rice cake (see pages 37–39)

puttu kuti vessel in which rice cake is steamed

puzhakkal ari boiled rice

puzhiangiathu boiled

Sadya vegetarian meal served at festivals and weddings, traditionally eaten on banana leaves

sarkara jaggery or unrefined cane sugar

shikakai soap nut

thera mango fruit leather (see pages 184–185)

thiyal vegetable dish prepared with roasted coconut and tamarind (see page 61)

thoran vegetables cooked with ground coconut (see page 52)

urali round-bottomed vessel traditionally made of bell metal

vanpayar red cow peas

varathathu fried

vattayappam steamed fermented rice cake (see page 144)

vazhakka raw banana

vellarai herb used for its anti-carcinogenic properties

villachayathu method of cooking

SUBSTITUTIONS

Ingredient	Substitution
coccum	tart green mango
fresh grated coconut	packaged shredded coconut
fresh coconut milk	packaged coconut milk and powder
thick coconut milk	undiluted packaged coconut milk
thin coconut milk	diluted packaged coconut milk
ghee	melted butter
jaggery	molasses or dark brown sugar
lime	lemon
toddy	active dry yeast

Vessels	Substitution
cheena chatti (Chinese cooking vessel)	wok
idiappam achu (*idiappam* maker)	fine ricer or vermicelli maker
puttu kuti (*puttu* steamer)	any type of steamer with teacups to fit in
paalappam chatti (*paalappam* vessel)	wok with a lid
urali	roasting pot or heavy skillet

NOTE

A recipe is essentially a guideline. When using a new recipe, it is important to read the entire process of cooking first. Around the world, people use different stoves, pots, and pans. The quality and size of ingredients may vary as nature doesn't give us perfectly consistent ingredients to work with. Hence there can be no precise universal standard for a recipe.

Many ingredients used in each recipe, including spices, oil, and salt, can be adjusted to suit one's taste. A gravy for a fish or chicken curry can be thick or thin and the water or coconut milk added can be adjusted to taste. As someone once said, "cooking is not a passive endeavour." Tastings, testings, and adjustments as you cook will give you the best results, especially when trying an unfamiliar cuisine.

The various members of my family whose recipes are featured here have added their distinct touches to the foods they create. I can hear my two grandmothers, my mother-in-law, a couple of aunts, and even my mother banter about my recipe for Kerala Chicken Curry or the classic Yesterday's Fish Curry and perhaps disown it. "Not from MY branch of the family," each would say.

BIBLIOGRAPHY

Ayyar, Ananthakrishna, Krishna, L. *Anthropology of the Syrian Christians*. Cochin Government Press, Ernakulam,1926.

Menon, K. P. Padmanabha. *History of Kerala, Notes on Visschers, Letters from Malabar*, Volume 1. Ernakulam, 1924.

Thomas, P. *Christianity in India and Pakistan*. George Allen and Unwin, London, 1954.

The Encyclopaedia Brittanica, Fourteenth Edition. Encyclopaedia Brittanica Inc., London, 1929.

Woodcock, George. *Kerala, A Portrait of The Malabar Coast*. Faber and Faber, London, 1967.

RESOURCES

Indian grocery stores across the U.S. stock most of the ingredients used in these recipes and will also get special ingredients for you on request. You can locate an Indian grocery store in your area on the following website: www.thokalath.com.

About the Author

Lathika George is a Bombay-born Syrian Christian who moved to Kerala during her teens. A culinary enthusiast, she has studied home science and creative writing. She and her husband reside in Kodaikanal in South India, where she runs a landscape design firm which specializes in hill station gardens.

INDEX

Acknowledgments

I would like to thank the many people who assisted and guided me through the writing of this book: my daughter and editor, Rajni George, who made it a reality; my sister, Latha George Pottenkulam, who both illustrated and helped shape the book; Tamar and Bruce DeJong as well as Jayashree Kumar for reading and editing my manuscripts—your valuable suggestions are much appreciated; thanks also to my friends P. Vasudev and Minoo and Schezarine Avari for coming to my rescue—"from the demon computer."

Many thanks to Dr. M. K. James for lending a unique perspective with his fascinating account of the early Syrian Christians.

I am also grateful to my publisher, George Blagowidow, who suggested I write this book and to editorial director, Priti Gress, for seeing it through.

My gratitude also goes out to Madhur Jaffrey for her invaluable advice.

A big thank you to my friends and family for sharing your photographs, memories, and recipes; my cousins Binny George Kollamkulam, who prepared the delicious food in the photographs, and Reenie and Antony Tharakan—you opened your home and hearth to us. (The traditional kitchen pictured on the cover is the hub of their ancestral home in Thycattassery.)

Finally, I am thankful to my children—Rajni, Roopa and Resham—and to my husband, George, for believing me to be "the best cook in the world."